ART
IN
THE
AGE
OF
RISK

NICOLAS CALAS was born and educated in Greece. He came to the United States in 1940 and became a citizen in 1945. During World War II Dr. Calas worked in the Office of War Information, and after the war he was associated with Research in Contemporary Cultures, a Columbia University Project headed by Dr. Margaret Mead. He is the author of several books: *Confound the Wise* (1943), *Primitive Heritage* (in collaboration with Margaret Mead, 1953), and *The Peggy Guggenheim Collection of Modern Art* (in collaboration with Elena Calas, 1967). Dr. Calas regularly contributes articles to *Arts Magazine* and *Art International* and is Associate Professor of Art at Fairleigh Dickinson University.

Art in the Age of Risk is the first in a projected series of volumes called "Documents in Modern Art Criticism."

ART IN THE AGE OF RISK

and Other Essays

NICOLAS CALAS

A Dutton Paperback

New York   E. P. Dutton & Co., Inc.   1968

for Lolya

Published simultaneously in Canada by
Clarke, Irwin and Company Limited, Toronto and Vancouver.

Library of Congress Catalogue Card Number: 68-28885

First Edition

CONTENTS

INTRODUCTION

Nicolas Calas is a critic of modern art who does not lend himself to simple categorization. He was associated in the Thirties with André Breton and the Surrealists. He has been a perpetual champion of the new; he wrote, in an earlier volume, "Let us change the past and transform the future! Let us fill them with the new images of our desires!"[1] Calas has written extensively on many subjects. He has published poetry and written on anthropology. His writings on Surrealism, Surrealist criticism, myths, memory, psychoanalysis, and the painter Hieronymous Bosch have acquired the status of critical documents. As art critic for *The Village Voice* Calas became one of the most widely read of modern-art critics, advocating a new and broad type of activism for art and a renewed vitality for criticism itself. His first published collection of criticism in English, *Confound the Wise,* has influenced numerous new-generation writers and thinkers. Calas has consistently sought to reveal the larger implications of art and the deepest meanings held within the art statement. His approach has been broad and has involved a wide field of learning; he has consistently managed to avoid the parochial.

The writings in this volume are largely devoted to the criticism of modern art. This does not imply, however, that the book contains a narrow range of ma-

[1] Nicolas Calas, *Confound the Wise,* New York: Arrow Editions, 1942, p. 82.

terial and subjects. Quite the contrary: Calas brings a broad humanist background to his searching discussions of a wide variety of problems growing out of modern art.

It would be a pity if the audience for *Art in the Age of Risk* were to be limited to those actively involved in the art world. While the artist, art critic, and student of art will find much of important interest in this book, so also will the political scientist, the educator, and the sociologist—as well as the general observer— interested in a perceptive and highly stimulating investigation into the special problems faced by a self-critical culture in turmoil.

Another critic who has shown concern for the condition of modern criticism and who has offered thoughts concerning the possibility of viable art criticism is Lucy Lippard. In one essay she writes (about the new critic): ". . . it is important for him to have some contact with the artist. There are dissenters who feel that the dangers of knowing an artist personally outweigh the advantages of a stimulating dialogue. . . . On the contrary, the most valid reason for contact between critic and artist is that the critic becomes close enough to the art-making experience to understand and tolerate, as well as admire, the whole complex situation in which the artist operates; he becomes familiar enough to criticize instead of simply to like or dislike."[2] Calas would be the first to agree with these remarks. In this volume Calas writes specifically about several artists; he knows all of them closely. His remarks on the Existentialist illustrations represented by the work of Barnett Newman are the result of a lengthy and close study of both the artist and his art. His interpretations of the works of Al Held reveal an intimate knowledge of artist, art, and ambiance. In his article on Robert Rauschenberg, Calas considers far more than just the artist's painting. History, poetry, philosophy, and humor all play a part in this critique.

In an essay entitled "Description Is Not Enough," reprinted in this volume, Nicolas Calas writes: ". . . when we view the work (of art) in terms of a consumption sequence, we feel obliged to describe it as if we were writing a lengthy invoice for a pedantic client or selling culture to students. Art being the expression of the intrinsic, the great work of art is a revelation sudden and indescribable because impenetrable." Today, it is common to categorize art critics as belonging, more or less, in one of two camps: the "descriptive," and the "humanistic." Recently, Mr. Bates-Lowry, the new director of the Museum of Modern Art, is reported to have said (concerning art critics and historians of our time): "Very few have attempted to redefine the broad general statements about the history of art in so far as it can tell us something about the history of mankind."[3] Surprisingly, this statement represents a relatively uncommon view toward the function of the art critic and art historian, even though it may not differ markedly from the traditional approach to the discipline that has been handed down to us through the history of Western art criticism. In his statement Bates-Lowry takes a clear stand. He opposes the "descriptive" type of art writing. He goes on to say: "You train someone to do a mammoth dissertation. Rarely do they attempt to talk about the quality of painting or how it relates to the society that produced it. People who are to be interpreters of art to the public have had their sights turned away from the important areas. It's all description and no interpretation."[4] Thus Mr. Bates-Lowry lines himself up squarely with a school of art criticism that has its beginnings in ancient Greece and Rome.

[3] *The New York Times,* February 22, 1968.
[4] *Ibid.*

Xenocrates, for example, carried criticism beyond simple descriptive and journalistic reporting. He wrote a treatise designed to give advice and to establish principles for painters and sculptors. He attempted to establish a relationship between artistic judgment, on one hand, and the art work itself, on the other. By so doing he prepared the way for a new humanistic discipline. His approach was markedly different from that of Polycleitos who wrote exclusively on problems concerning proportion and the human figure. This distinction between the approach to art criticism found in the writing of both Polycleitos and Xenocrates, is a distinction that is still very much with us today.

Throughout the Early Christian and Medieval centuries there was a continual process of philosophic development within the area of aesthetics. Many of the modern ideas that evolved during the Renaissance were anticipated during this period. Vasari, Alberti, and Cennini are but three of the numerous Renaissance writers who contributed to the foundations of our modern aesthetic. Toward the end of the Renaissance we find other writers pursuing the humanist approach to art criticism. In 1584 the Lombardian Mannerist painter Gian Paolo Lomazzo wrote his "Treatise on the Art of Painting," in which he emphasizes by an argument that varies between empirical observation and abstract concept that art is both an imitation of nature and the expression of ideas. In a more modern—and humorous—vein, Nicolas Calas has expressed the thought: "Poetry should be seen and not heard; music should be as hard as bones; painting should think."

In 1762 Johann Hamann maintained that spontaneity and imagination are everything in art, that genius is against all the rules, the "truth," the systems, the foundations of art.[5] And in 1797, in opposition to the

[5] Lionello Venturi, *History of Art Criticism*, New York: Dutton Paperbacks, 1964, p. 169.

rigid classical formalism of the day, William Henry Wackenroder directed the attention of the observer to the artist's way of feeling. Thus yet another dimension was added to the field of humanistic art criticism.

It is in more recent times, however, that liberal and humanistic ideas about the nature and purpose of art criticism received their greatest encouragement. With the mid-nineteenth century liberation from the classicism represented by David and Ingres in France, we find a renewal of the type of criticism that champions the new and accepts the relative, as opposed to the absolute, in art judgment. And by 1864 it was no longer unusual to consider art as challenge and polemic. One popular newspaper critic, writing on Manet's painting *Bullfight* notes: "Here is another victim of the viciousness of public morals, a voluntary victim stretched out in the center of a bull ring at one end of a vast arena . . ." ". . . His painting is a kind of challenge, and he apparently wants to exasperate the public like the picadors in his Spanish bullfight jabbing arrows with multicolored ribbons into the neck of a savage adversary."[6] Thus painting is seen as a provocative medium threatening and questioning prevailing values.

Even earlier, in 1855, Charles Baudelaire spoke out against a system for aesthetic judgment that he found inevitably debilitating. He wrote: "Like all my friends I have tried more than once to lock myself up within a system in order to preach there at my ease. But a system is a kind of damnation which forces one to perpetual recantation: it is always necessary to be inventing a new one, and the drudgery involved is a cruel punishment."[7] By remarks such as these, written with both humor and extraordinary perception, Baudelaire repudiated the lingering classical temperament

[6] George Heard Hamilton, *Manet and His Critics,* New Haven: Yale University Press, 1954, p. 60.

[7] Charles Baudelaire, *The Mirror of Art,* New York: Doubleday & Company, 1956, p. 195.

toward art and interpretation, and paved the way for acceptance and understanding of the radical new art of Manet and the Impressionists.

Baudelaire preferred Delacroix over Ingres, and he found much lacking in the art of Ingres. He pointed out, in an essay on Ingres written in 1855 that: ". . . the duty of criticism should be to seek to penetrate deep into the temperament and activating motives of each artist rather than to attempt to analyze and describe each work minutely."[8] Baudelaire noted that the Beautiful is always strange and that mere stylistic problems should be held subordinate to the larger mysteries of art and the art process. Baudelaire's views go a considerable distance toward preparing the groundwork for an Existentialist and logical positivist view of art—one that is shared by many art critics today. In a similar vein Eugène Delacroix wrote in his Journal in 1822: "There is in me something that is often stronger than my body, which is often enlivened by it. In some people the inner spark scarcely exists. I find it dominant in me. Without it I should die, but it will consume me (doubtless I speak of imagination, which masters and leads me)."[9]

In the twentieth century we find numerous major steps toward the development of a humanist criticism for art. Wilhelm Worringer's *Abstraction and Empathy* was widely read during the early years of the century. And T. E. Hulme concerned himself with the opposed conceptions ". . . of the nature of man, which in reality lie at the root of our more concrete beliefs—the Religious and the Humanist."[10] While Hulme attempted to reconcile the two natures of man,

[8] *Ibid.*, p. 202.

[9] Elizabeth Holt (Ed.), *From the Classicists to the Impressionists,* New York: Doubleday & Company, 1966, p. 153.

[10] T. E. Hulme, *Speculations,* New York: Harcourt, Brace, 1961, p. 57.

he was not entirely successful. He did, however, clarify the Humanist view, as he saw it, and defined along with it the modern capitalistic reality. At the same time it became clear that a Marxist view, in opposition to the prevalent capitalistic one, would prove a viable and meaningful key to the practical problems delineated by the new art.

One nineteenth-century predecessor of modern criticism—a critic whose writings may still prove of considerable interest to the New-Left artist and critic —is William Morris. His connection with the Pre-Raphaelite school is well known, but some of his art criticism is not so well known. Morris was deeply involved in the vital problems of art on one hand, and the happiness of the people on the other. In his essay entitled "Art for All," Morris wrote: "Unless something or other is done to give all men some pleasure for the eyes and rest for the mind in the aspect of their own and their neighbor's houses, until the contrast is less disgraceful between the fields where beasts live and the streets where men live, I suppose that the practice of the arts must be mainly kept in the hands of a few highly cultivated men who can go often to beautiful places, whose education enables them in the contemplation of the past glories of the world, to shut out from their view the every day squalors that the most of men move in."[11] Art criticism with social consciousness, while not entirely new, had never been proposed with the determination and, indeed, the practical application exhibited by Morris.

A new type of art criticism that includes a different approach to interpretation as well as a new definition of the responsibilities of the critic to the artist and culture of his time can hardly be evaluated without

[11] William Morris, *Selections from the Prose Works* (A. H. R. A. Ball, Ed.), Cambridge: Cambridge University Press, 1931, p. 168.

consideration of numerous developments in related fields. For instance, Freud's psychoanalytic observations on the sexuality of Leonardo and his interpretations of the *Moses* by Michelangelo are important documents, and the possibility of a psychoanalytic approach to the problems of art impressed both the Dadists and Surrealists. Thus, awesome responsibilities have been thrust upon both the modern critic *and* modern artist. As Kandinsky pointed out in 1946: "It is as if the artist was God, designing and creating new worlds in His own likeness."[12]

Naturally, there are many ways of looking at and criticizing art. The logical positivist will be satisfied simply to experience the work itself. His empirical method leaves little room for any further conclusion. Then there is the historical approach in which art is seen exclusively in historical terms; even new art. Another view greets new art with enthusiasm simply, or perhaps mostly, because it *is* new. In this instance one should not try to explain the art because one isn't really sure what art is anyway. Thus the critic is faced with the choice either of constantly making mistakes or playing it safe.

It would seem that now is the time for taking chances and making mistakes. Only change can, at this time, avert disaster. Both the critic and the artist are in a position to effect this change, but according to many observers, neither is moving fast enough, or is even moving in the right direction. The art critic Gene Swensen points out: "The art world can and has played a major role in averting thus far the inevitable social and cultural revolution which our oligarchy— the last bastion against the Bolshevik rabble—so fears. . . . A different approach may end up as sys-

[12] Wassily Kandinsky, *On the Spiritual in Art* (Public Comments made in the Museum of Non-Objective Painting in New York City, from January to April, 1946), New York: The Solomon Guggenheim Foundation, 1946, p. 127.

tematic social realism, but what could be worse than Neo-Modern? The time to chart an alternative to the neo-modern tyranny is now."[13] In another article, Swensen notes: "A revolution, however, needs its artists, perhaps most of all. And none of us has been doing enough. Let there arise in our midst a cry for Freedom: of spirit, of person, of social conscience."[14]

In his essay "Surrealist Perspective" in this volume, Calas points out that Surrealist works are intended to disturb, not appease. He goes on to say: ". . . the Surrealist goal is unrest, not peace." "We have sufficiently represented reality; it is time to transform it" would be the Surrealist counterpart of Marx's famous dictum: "We have sufficiently explained the world; it is time to transform it." However Calas does not limit this view to the Surrealists exclusively. If we encourage change, if change is a goal, then the possibility of error is increased enormously. In his essay "Art in the Age of Risk" Calas points out: "In the age of risk success is the criterion of the good . . . lack of success cannot be equated with evil, and responsibility for the slave's failure may be thrown upon the master . . . there is no royal way of discovering truth; there is only the empirical way of finding out facts."

Calas clearly supports those who show disgust for the traditional institutions in art, with their remoteness, sterility, and irrelevance, and he clearly advocates the type of interpretation that relates art to the human condition. His attitude is not, alas, prevalent in art criticism today. He recognizes that revolution on the campus is only one of many revolutions that are directed against the obsolete institutions found in our modern world. The art museum has been relatively safe from this type of dramatic confrontation because it was thought that art itself contained built-in revo-

[13] Gene Swensen, *The New York Free Press*, April 25, 1968, p. 9.
[14] *Ibid.*, June 20, 1968, p. 6.

lution. That art *is* revolution—and especially that modern art is never establishment—has been taken for granted. However, the modern museum today has proven that art—modern art—is not necessarily revolution. Indeed, it frequently can be both academic and Establishment. Much of modern art today is art for the art historians.

Calas is aware of the dangers to art created by the historically minded museum curator. He has observed the museum becoming a laboratory for the university and its department of art history. In a critique of the exhibition "Dada, Surrealism, and Their Heritage" (Museum of Modern Art, 1968) Calas wrote: "The Museum of Modern Art is the depository of major works of the twentieth century and as such is invaluable for the artist and the scholar but, like all official and semi-official organizations, it harms more than it helps when it thrusts its weight around. In the age of technocracy we take it for granted that managers of museums disregard intellectual problems. The programs of museums have become as meaningless as those of the big political parties; they are but advertising slogans."[15] Thus the problem can be put this way: does art seen in different positions (i.e. exhibitions) demand different conclusions?

One reason for the reluctance of modern critics to take necessary chances in the service of more meaningful art criticism is a concern for and a fear of the judgment of history. It is imperative that history judge us favorably. This concern for posterity's verdict is frequently responsible for the scope, intent, and content of many contemporary exhibitions as well as critical appraisals. In his book *Manet and His Critics,* Hamilton inadvertently illustrates this concern. One is amused to read the carefully documented and picturesquely presented verbiage of Manet's con-

[15] Nicolas Calas, "Surrealist Heritage?," *Arts Magazine,* Vol. 42, No. 5, March, 1968, p. 24.

temporary critics who, for the most part, didn't give a damn for the judgment of history. Because of their appalling lack of historical perspective, they appear very foolish indeed. It is difficult to imagine any serious artist or critic today who does not work with a good grasp of the history of Western art and thought. But because of our belief that concern for the contemporary condition will almost inevitably be followed by the censure of history, we respond with a devotion to historical principles and a slavish preoccupation with historical precedent and license. As Calas observes in his essay "Anarchy and Edgar Wind": "But of all the gods man invented to free himself from anxiety, none proved more demanding than History. . . . to the art historian's analysis of the symbolic meaning of the language of art, the champion of modern art opposes the structural analysis of the artist's statement; to the scholar's reference to history, he will oppose the modern anthropologist's cultural patterns; and to the humanist's ethical values, the Promethean freedom from responsibility."

The role of the serious critic of modern art is one of continual challenge and self-searching; it is also a role of inestimable worth to all those who cherish the artist as a member and interpreter of the infinite facets of our modern society. In this book Nicolas Calas proves to be one who assumes his role with great insight, with real concern for the larger and more spacious values of art in the modern world, and with a felicity of style and wit that affords the reader much stimulation.

Gregory Battcock

ILLUSTRATIONS

I.
CONTINUANCE

SURREALIST INTENTIONS*

*Is it not Surrealism's great merit to have made the spectator pay **more** attention to the conscious meaning of pictures?*

A shift of emphasis from the unconscious to the conscious is unavoidable every time we pass from the field of research to that of communication. Psychoanalysis, like all sciences which deal with diachronic data, looks for what is hidden back of the present. The writing of a poem and the painting of a picture fall into the category of means of communication by which a certain type of relationship is established between the communicator and others.

Confessions

I would call *expository* the communicated information dealing with data that are not unknown to the public, and *revelatory* that dealing with facts mostly or totally unknown. If the revelation refers to events concerning the affective life of the communicator himself, it is a *confession*.

There are four types of confession: the *judicial*, the *religious*, the *literary*, and the *psychoanalytic*. Certain modern forms of writing, such as the stream of consciousness used by Dostoevski and Joyce, and which

* Reprinted from *Trans/Formation*, 1950.

the Surrealists call automatic writing, resemble the psychoanalytic confession. But does this comparison imply that the Surrealist confession has ceased to be a literary one? Before answering, one should explore the difference between psychoanalytic and religious confession. Comparison with judicial confession, however, would only be confusing, as the purpose of the latter is to *seal* the fate of the guilty instead of *raising* his hopes—which last is the objective of both psychoanalysis and religious confession.

As has been excellently said by Victor White,[1] confession refers to sin, that is to say, to "the evil men do" —*malum culpae*, while the psychoanalytic confession refers to "the evil men suffer"—*malum poenae*. A psychoanalyst could brush aside this distinction on the ground that the evil men do is, in the last analysis, caused by an evil they have previously suffered (which is but a way of posing once more the vexing problem of free will only to dismiss it in the name of psychological naturalism). If correct, it would follow that the artist should be evaluated according to what his unconscious urges lead him to write rather than in accordance with what he says.

A major part of the writing done by the Surrealists in the twenties was produced on the basis of an absolute faith in psychological determinism. The purpose of automatic writing was to enable the artist to feed his work with the stream of unconscious associations. However significant this phase of development may have been for the self-education of the Surrealist writers and painters, its contribution to art and literature remained secondary, and no Surrealist can honestly claim that his major works were ever done purely automatically. Nevertheless these unsuccessful

[1] Victor White: "The Analyst and the Confessor," in *The Commonweal*, July 23, 1948.

experiments are worth considering. Had it been found that the inner core or essence of art could be reduced to automatic associations, the artist would have been turned into a seismograph of his soul, which is tantamount to the denial of talent and art, or the assertion that *all free flow of unconscious thought is art.*

Surrealism, which started its career as a successor of Dada, did actually advocate the abolition of art. If the purpose of writing or painting is reduced to the outpouring of the unconscious on paper or canvas, the objective of art would be to transform reality into the bed of dreams.

It is one thing, however, to say that by means of a conscious description of an experience such as a dream we shall *introduce* the contents of an unconscious activity into the realm of reality; and another to *substitute unconscious methods of expression* for the reality by which we communicate the unconscious contents. The former is done by an ordinary description of dreams; the latter is what automatic writing *claims* to do when, instead of pouring unconscious content into a mold of reality, it replaces this mold with an unrecognizable form.

The mold of reality into which the unreal must be set is language; the unrecognizable form is made of the meaningless sentences that have poured from the soul under the dictation of the unconscious.

Surrealism

If the artist's purpose is the negation of reality, he could approach this goal better by substituting drugs for writing or painting, thereby plunging himself more fully into fantasy, or by becoming an anarchist and devoting himself to the destruction of an abhorred reality: society. But Surrealism has always claimed that it wished to reform society—which presupposes a recognition of its value. Members of the human society understand each other by the use of signs. Language being the basic means of interpersonal communication, all interpersonal methods of communication, such as painting and poetry, must be adapted to a linguistic structure; they are founded on the *linguistic level of reality.*

As I see it, Surrealism does not purpose to abolish the linguistic reality of poets (anymore than it aims at abolishing society), but to reform it by introducing into its reality symbols obtained from dreams.

Surrealism can reform reality only by preventing the stream of unconscious associations, which it has allowed to pour out freely, from flooding the reality of language. The Surrealist must know when he should close the dam that keeps the unconscious under his control. Using his judgment he must decide when to stop speaking automatically. There is in the creative process a point which even the Surrealist cannot bypass and at which he arrives when he chooses to close the gates. Only he can decide at what moment this should be done. Upon his choice will depend what proportion of unknown or unconscious symbols will be mixed with the known linguistic symbols.

Being responsible for his choice, the Surrealist is responsible for what he communicates, as the function of language is to establish communication.[2] Even psychoanalysis, the latest invented method of confession, is based upon freedom of choice, and construed on the premise of the analysand's free will. If the analysand does not choose to communicate, the analyst remains powerless. Like the confessor, the utmost he can do is to help the sufferer help himself, which implies that confession takes place this side of freedom.

[2] See the writer's "Iconolatry and Iconoclasm," in *College Art Journal*, New York, Winter, 1949–50.

The Western emphasis on free will is reflected in justice: the courts tend to be more lenient to that offender who confesses his guilt. To plead guilty shows a will to reform. In *Crime and Punishment* Dostoevski has forcefully illustrated this point and described how, through his will to improve, a man can become strong enough to persevere along the path of reform even after he has been condemned.

Although religious and psychoanalytic confessions may often go deeper than literary confessions, they are less perfect: just as the teacher of a language helps us to communicate our feelings by indicating the "proper" meaning and usage of words, so the psychoanalyst "teaches" the patient the true meaning of symbols that he pours out in a stream of unconscious associations; so the confessor "teaches" the penitent the meaning, or implications, of his sins. The purpose of these "lessons" is to help the individual to communicate with his neighbors—through psychoanalysis; or with God—through confession.

The difference between the confessor and the analyst is analogous to that between the teacher imparting a foreign language to an adult and a teacher who instructs children how to talk. The priest teaches a "foreign language," the language of prayer, for confessions must be finally addressed to a "foreign" person: God. The psychoanalyst treats us as children who do not know the meaning of their emotions; like children, we can understand them ourselves only by learning what meaning others attribute to them. This implies the knowledge of language, and calls for an adaptation to language, as it is only through it that we can communicate with others in terms they can understand.

The Message

Unlike the patient or the penitent, the mature artist, whether Surrealist or not, is not hampered by "communication difficulties," and is able to communicate with his public directly, without the assistance of a teacher. The readers are not expected to tell the writer what is the meaning of the symbols he uses; on the contrary it is the reader who expects the communicated message to have meaning and to contain a "truth."

This message, as is the case in art, can *refer* to an emotion; but the emotion cannot be *part* of the message which, delivered linguistically, consists merely of signs. Some signs have a symbolic meaning and can be associated by the reader with his own emotions, through which he can identify himself with the communicator's emotions, but the message or content of the work he sees or reads remain symbolic. *The reader who cannot comprehend certain symbols has the right to assume that he can learn their meaning just as he learns the meanings of signs used in another language or the signs of the language of music or mathematics. But the signs and the symbols must refer to a given code.*

If the communicator himself cannot refer them to any known language, it is as if he had not used language at all and had therefore never formulated his ideas or feelings; it is as if he had not spoken— the implication being that he should have either kept silent or have learned to speak before writing or painting. To use words without knowing their symbolic meaning (which is the automatic writing process) is analogous to using unfamiliar foreign words, and constitutes a *misuse* rather than a use of language. One cannot therefore speak of communication when confronted with a work that does not have conscious meaning.

The Mask

If he is to find an audience, the Surrealist, like all artists, must follow certain laws *that in the last analy-*

sis are linguistic. Communications hold our interest either for *what* is said or for *how* it is said, either for the *value* of the information contained or for the *attractiveness* of the presentation. The latter is the artistic component of the communication. If the public feels that the information contained in the communication is not new and has been *better* presented in an earlier version they will have no reason to pay any attention to the later work.

Viewed from the angle of what is said, the communication is either an exposition of carefully made *observations* or a revelation obtained through *insight.* The less a communication appears to be an exposition, the stronger will be the demand to have it presented in an attractive way: communication through insight is of the order of *showing the hidden.* The false artist is one who exhibits his showmanship (mannerisms), and attempts to compensate the lack of insight by adding superfluous decorations. Actually, however, instead of showing what is hidden, the artist—all artists —replaces the hidden with a substitute which he embellishes to make it more attractive so that the spectator, charmed, should come to expect that what is hidden will actually be shown. What we are actually shown, however, is a mask.

Art Is Enigmatic

Art is a form of communication that insinuates. We *expect* the artist to have more to say than what he communicated, and to *suspect* that what he said was a subterfuge for hiding something. Hence the interest in the artist's intentions that led him to produce or not to produce a work, and the deep feeling of frustration one feels when an artist dies young or substitutes his eloquent enigmas with the eloquent silence of a Rimbaud. To understand the *significance* of a work of art means to be more interested in the artist's intentions than in his communication.

It follows that it is not sufficient to say that the work of art must have linguistic meaning as it is a medium by means of which a relation, through perceptual contact, is established between the observer and a hiding place. The "place" from which the work of art emerges is situated within the communication and is referred to as mind, psyche, or heart. Through artistic communication one can establish a *deeper* rapport with the artist than one can by a *closer* contact, as for instance through conversation.

The Gift

The work of art is primarily a communication, but it is also more: we expect the artist to say *better* what others may have already said. This *improvement* is obtained by *doing* something to the medium (language). The transformation of the "raw material" into a work of art, the "gift" to present "beautifully" what others have said "crudely," to be "poetic" where others are prosaic, constitutes the artist's *gift* to the community.

The making of a work of art requires *labor*, that is, expense of energy, and involves fatigue of mind and body—one must take *pains* if something is to be done well.

Rationalization of pain has played a most important role in the elaboration of the cultural values of the Western world. An aura of glory surrounds that pain which has been willfully accepted in a spirit of *sacrifice*. In sacrifice there is an element of *satisfaction*, that is, of "the willing acceptance and performance of some task imposed as compensation and as a token of good faith and willingness to accept the penal consequence of sin" (V. White). When reinterpreted in aesthetic terms, satisfaction is the willing acceptance of artistic tasks as a compensation for deep-felt anxiety and the willingness to communicate one's suffering to one's fellowmen. The artist is willing to take pains, and the community recognizes his sacrifice, his labor, his suffering, by *accepting* his work as a token of good faith, that is, as a *gift*. One could add parenthetically that the popular belief that artists are not avaricious and spend money freely corresponds to the need to place the artist in the position of a donor.

The donor gives in order to enter into the good graces of the beneficiary, the way the penitent gives to receive forgiveness from his God, or the way the lover gives to acquire favors from the beloved. But the artist is a particular kind of donor, for what he gives is a work that is not simply a token of good faith, for it contains a message. The message, as it were, confirms the gift by convincing us that the donor is sincere, for what he says is true, in the sense that the message has been delivered in good faith. In the last analysis the message, like the gift, must be appreciated in relation to the artist's good intentions.

The profoundest works of art are those related to the most hidden intentions. The deeper the artist plunges into himself through introspection, the further he moves away from the assurance of facts, the nearer he will approach the ambiguity of dreams. To convictions obtained through inquiries concerning the facts of reality he will oppose the doubts of his own emotions. In place of self-assurance and certitude he will offer doubt and anxiety. It is anxiety that he will *express*. But the *subject* of confession can only be sin or guilt (unless we consider it a sin to be anxious, for then it is the sin of anxiety that we confess), which is tantamount to saying that the artist does not actually confess. What he does do is to give form to anxiety by substituting an enigma for it.

The artist does not want to expose his sins or perversions, but to convey his anxiety. To make his anxiety understood he will describe conditions that will evoke in our minds feelings similar to his own. This is why often a metaphorical expression of anxiety achieved through the description of fictitious circumstances creates better conditions for communication of anxiety than does an accurate report of the actual conditions under which it had been experienced. The greatest confessions of anxiety are the false or fictitious confessions such as those Dostoevski made in *The Possessed, Crime and Punishment,* and *The Brothers Karamazov.* What we want is the enigma, not the truth; the beautiful confession, not the true confession. To the extent that Augustine and Rousseau falsified their confessions they are sincere.

The Church, aware that confession requires *satisfaction* at the accomplishment of some task, insists that it should be followed by contrition, that is to say, "the turning of the will from sin to God" (V. White). If we substitute anxiety for sin, then we can see how satisfaction can be obtained by contrition or *insight* into suffering, and satisfaction by the accomplishment of the artistic task and the making of the enigma.

The "turning of the will" of the artist through contrition involves a turning away from the specific circumstances that caused pain, and the concentration of his will upon the task of communication. The ambiguity between personal suffering and impersonal circumstances can only help to heighten that enigmatic quality which makes us ask that art be "truer to life than life itself."

If the artist did not work in good faith and in a spirit of contrition, if his basic motivation was not to give but to *receive*, if money or fame were his real motivations, then his work is no more a gift and therefore is not a work of art. One of the basic functions of the critic consists in finding out whether a work is genuine and has been made in good faith, for otherwise the community has been cheated.

The Dandy

When in our examination of the work of art our interest is directed toward the donor's intentions rather than toward the communicator's message, the only information we can expect to obtain is related to what the artist *failed to do*. What he has *done* we will find in his biography, what he *says* by studying his work. Intentions will reveal his most secret desires and help us understand which ones were never realized either in deeds or in words.

The theory of intentions is a theory of the failure to act out (to do or communicate). Surrealism, by using symbols borrowed from the vocabulary of dreams, has indicated that the Surrealist messages are concerned with the failure to *do*.

This explains why the models of the Surrealists are neither heroes nor villains, who are judged by their deeds, but beings whom we judge by their dreams, as Breton's *Nadja*, Nerval's *Aurelia*, Kafka's "K," Charlie Chaplin's impersonations. In Surrealist art, the artist *viewed as dreamer* becomes the subject of art.

The need for a shift of emphasis from the objective world of reality to the subjective world of the self in art was keenly felt, although already ambiguously expressed, by Oscar Wilde when he said that he put his talent in his art and his genius in his life. The artist who concentrates all his energy on his art no longer understands life and has turned himself into a workman, thereby putting the emphasis on *making* rather than on *giving*, on the pain of necessity rather than on the pain of contrition, on the pleasure of reward rather than on the pleasure of satisfaction.

If the artist is to express his inner self with all its anxieties, what he does must be related to love and pleasure rather than to work and duty. Hence the pain that the artist goes through and expresses in his work of art is the pain of contrition, while the pleasure is derived from the feeling of relief that it is not a product of work and that he was free to *play* with his work as a child can play with its toys. In all great works of art there is a combination of joy and grief stemming from the joy of not having to work and the pain of being anxious.

If one does not put one's genius in one's art, then one risks putting one's talent at the service of necessity. Unless, of course, one has no genius, and puts one's talent in one's life. Just as the artist imitates anxiety through enigmas so he imitates work in his "play." He plays the role of a worker, which would suggest that he is an actor, although he is not an actor because acting is not his work. He does not play the role of an actor the way the actor plays the role of a hero, but like the actor he enjoys showing himself different from what he is. It is as if he wore an actor's mask to play himself.

The artist is different from both the hero and the worker in that he has no profession and belongs to the type described so well by Baudelaire: the dandy. *The artist is a dandy; the artist is a donor.* The dandy is a person who *owns* nothing, neither power nor money, and *owes* nothing, neither gratitude nor service; therefore the gifts that he gives have no value—a meaning which is implied in the idea that art is useless.

The Player

The feeling that art is useless heightens the artist's Hamletian anxiety which can be overcome only by greater devotion to play. The Surrealist interest in playing games helps to remind the artist of the danger of exchanging the independence of the player for the servitude of the worker. A work of art can lose its freshness if it bears the traces of too much work. A work of art fades when the public dissects it with the labor of scholarship; when viewing work as priceless, one is led to believe that it involves more work than money could buy. The role of the artist qua dandy is to play with masterpieces and add moustaches to *Mona Lisa*.

To play means to have faith in chance; nothing could be more artistic than to allow chance (instead of work) to complete one's work, as Marcel Duchamp did when he permitted the accident that shattered his glass painting.

The artist should achieve that state of grace in which one overcomes the vain satisfaction of solving purely aesthetic problems. This the mystics do when they renounce art and pursue through prayer a soliloquy with God. The *exercise of the attention* achieved through pursuit of God being the positive element of prayer, it follows that for the artist the exercise of the attention will be followed in the field of games. For the true artist, like Marcel Duchamp, a soliloquy is established over a chessboard rather than in front of an icon—an attitude that can only lead one to become aware of one's own limitations in time, for, like toys, we are destined to total destruction.

This does not imply that because the artist uses pawns he must allow himself to be used as a pawn by those who, intent on drawing attention to their work, focus their gaze at a given moment of their career upon someone who, like Picasso, happens to be the object of general attention.

The supreme message of art as conveyed by those who have put their genius in their life is to help us realize that failure, failure to solve the enigma of life, is more important than to find successful solutions.

HEIRS U.S.A.*

Hindsight is needed to understand a new point of view. Only that which makes us feel we missed something is truly new. Works of art are precious because irreplaceable: the new can never replace the previously created. Conversely, the old is never large enough to make the new unnecessary. The term "avant-garde," with all its connotations, political, social, and even scientific, remains delightfully misleading. Continuity is achieved by advancing from the unique to the unique in the vivifying atmosphere of the young, intent on asserting themselves and on imposing their point of view—a view which is a nuance of the past, not its contradiction.

Modern art is fortunately old enough for us to realize that its very existence depends on our capacity to re-experience in new terms—abstract, for instance—the ecstasy of a Monet or a Cézanne. If modern art were to be banned from our world, we would be impoverished; and, while the poor are made stronger than others through faith, those who appreciate the uniqueness of *Nude Descending a Staircase* or of *Pierrot Lunaire* endow existence with a value that no participation in a common cause, however lofty, provides.

From this egocentric standpoint only works that establish a new set of references between the being

* Reprinted from *Art News*, February, 1959.

and worlds can be missed. The rest is to be dismissed for its verbosity and beauty.

The artist with a calling listens to strange voices and sets himself the task of translating the foreign terms of a science or a religion into paint. *Traduttore traditore!* Once upon a time the Surrealists believed they were betraying art when they in fact betrayed Freud. Art was to betray Surrealism, and this is where my story begins.

In the era of the Nazi persecution of man, a few Surrealists landed in New York, but their verb was coldly received. However, the act, or rather the gesture, the grand manner in which their paintings came into being fascinated the new vanguard. Abstract art certainly profited from the freedom Surrealism brought to painting by transforming the psychoanalytic free association into automatic tracings and the accidents of frottages. What the new vanguard rejected was the symbol that Surrealism had brandished as a challenge to the "formalism" of the Fauves and the Cubists. To the symbol the new school opposed the sign.

If the cloud is a sign of rain, and not a symbol of rain, so runs the argument, a set of signs and not a cluster of symbols is required to interpret phenomena. A sign is needed to warn the driver on the road that he is coming to a curve. The great merit of a Mondrian and a Kandinsky is to have made symbols unnecessary and brought into being an adult form of art.

The validity of establishing the distinction between sign and symbol cannot be seriously contested. It does not follow, however, that pictorial language should be deprived of the use of symbols. For instance, it is one matter for the prosaically minded tourist visiting the Tyrol to come upon a Crucifix at the crossroads and another for the local peasant who stops and makes the sign of the cross before the symbol of the presence of the deity. Likewise, at the op-

posite pole of the psychological spectrum, the shoe
fetishist charges with libido an object that for another
is perhaps nothing more than the sign of a woman's
presence. However, both crucifix and shoe when
touched by the artist can be transmuted into poetry.
Is this magic to be lost?

A transition from Surrealism to Abstract Expressionism was made by Matta. Realizing that by the time
he came upon the scene the muse of the unconscious
was muttering the same old story, Matta cleverly replaced the repressed microcosm with the unobtainable
macrocosm. A pupil of Le Corbusier, Matta found no
difficulty in transforming the architect's blueprints
into those of an outer space, a space that science
fiction had failed to imagine. Thanks to his astral
reticles, Matta's cartoons became cobwebs of Eros—
a grandiose undertaking that has not yet received all
the attention it deserves. Whether we are able or not
to see the fourth dimension in these futuramas is no
more the point than whether the twain are one color
in the *Grande Jatte*—the artist's achievements being
so often the consequence of miscalculations. Ever
since the Sixth Day creation consists in the creation of
errors.

Matta's loosened architectural designs provided
Gorky with the opportunity to reinterpret Miró *d'après
Cézanne* in terms of an automatic writing tutored by
a well-disciplined hand and supervised by a discern-
ing eye. Gorky's polyphonic Mirós justify the utterance
of an art student I once saw in Central Park drawing
the space between the branches when he said to me
that painting begins with Gorky.

Parallel to Gorky stands Pollock. The recent exhibition of his early work demonstrates that he had been
greatly encouraged by Masson's attempt to give to one
of Picasso's most striking forms—the triangle curved
by the wind of inspiration—the greater flexibility and

all the sinuosity of folds and ripples. Pollock's investigations led him to the discovery of a writing by means of which the fire of inspiration could be turned into melting colors which seduce by their vertiginous meanderings, by endless departures and returns to and from the world of fear-full existences and the tempting vacancy of universes.

Frottage, which Max Ernst had so forcefully trained into images, was reduced, much later, by the Tachisme of the Rive Droite into a forced Rorschach wherein images arise at the call of our vision.

Unlike the artist of the school of geometric abstractions, the Tachistes and the Expressionists are not committed to ostracizing the image. Long after he became famous, Pollock tried his hand at the representation of the human anatomy, and some of de Kooning's best known paintings consist of a series in which he applies his Abstract-Expressionist language to the praise of the woman.

Expressionists rediscovered what the empiricist found in philosophy: Abstraction does not consist, as the Euclidian-minded believed, in the emptying of a form of its contents, but in singling out an object. To use Reichenbach's forceful image: When a dog chooses its bone, it in fact abstracts it. Hence, if to a set of signs consisting of lines and colors the artist adds an image, treated as a specimen of a new set of signs, it would become another pictorial element when properly fitted into the pattern. This is precisely what Larry Rivers does.

Ever since Matisse painted a woman's face green—"when I run out of red I use blue" (Picasso)—it became possible to re-create the Pythagorean music of numbers and the color of vowels. William Hayter—the abstract Master ES of engraving—brought to life dislocated human figures through an original adaptation of frottage, and de Kooning dismembered the ego by shifting the boundaries of the body image, bathing it thereby in an aura of doubt—a *dédoublement* that has its counterpart in Samuel Beckett's *Molloy*.

Unlike them, Larry Rivers picked up a thread that leads back to what Matisse did when, in his interpretation of a woman seated in a chair, he disregarded all realistic taboos and systematically re-evaluated the colors in terms of purely plastic effects. Pursuing the experiment, Rivers dares to interchange a red patch and the head of a woman: while in one version the red patch is in the upper-right corner and the head in the center, in another painting, the red square appears in the center and the head in the upper-right corner. Recently in a sculpture he placed one of two mask-like disks upside down because "it looks better that way."

In Rivers' paintings the images are relaxed, and the canvas is brought surprisingly close to the sketchbook, making it thus possible to express many moods in one picture. How much an image can be freed from its reality is demonstrated by a painting in which Rivers translates the view of the houses seen through his studio window into an interior, achieved by replacing the transparency of atmosphere with a dense blue. Automatically the window, through which the woman across the street is seen looking out of her window, becomes that woman's chair.

Having been prepared by Abstract Expressionism to accept the irregularities of patterns (as contrasted to the basic harmony of asymmetrically set elements in geometric abstractions), it is no longer difficult to follow those who make the next step: the heightening of the accidental character of the pattern conveyed by the inclusion of images as accidents in the pattern. In *The Studio* Rivers presents his set of figures in doubles. What strange accident brings them twice there? It is hardly surprising that one of Rivers' best paintings should depict an accident. The story is told in a series of incidents. As in Jean Genêt's *Querelle de*

Larry Rivers. *Dutch Masters Presidents* relief, 1964. Oil
and collage on canvas mounted in wooden box. 98″ x
69½″ x 12″. Photograph courtesy of Marlborough-Gerson
Gallery, New York.

Brest, the sense of continuity has been broken up so as to increase the impact of the liberated incidents, liberated but not isolated as in Giotto or cartoons. The overall impression is one of an incompleteness that conveys the climate of accidents.

Attempts to depict hazardous speed recently made by Matta in his neo-Futurist paintings fail because of the constant increase in speed. What has not been eliminated and continues to fascinate is the accident's weight.

As the artist can buy ready-made colors instead of grinding them, so he can "buy" ready-made illustrations and compose a collage. If true abstraction consists in choosing the elements of the composition (and not in imitating the elements of a pre-existing image), there is no reason why the abstract artist cannot replace the painting of a surface by a painted or illustrated surface. With Robert Rauschenberg, painted surfaces fall into Abstract-Expressionist patterns emphasizing a sense of rawness akin to that which enabled de Kooning to tap beneath the skin of Fauvism. When, in Rauschenberg's *The Parlor,* a plane of faded red velvet is set against a glossy red paper, the velvet bleeds and the gloss coagulates. Instead of the hushed past, the evoked image is disembowled. Likewise, when a piece of lamé, dimmed by a streak of traffic yellow, bars all rapport between the athletic Michelangelo and the shy nymphet pasted on either side, the conveyed meaning is that the green light has not yet been turned on sex. All the details of Rauschenberg's "Combines" (objects) can be as easily read as a tattooed obelisk. It remains to understand what is happening to that fowl or that goat or those old boots, enthroned or encaged in the Combine.

What has happened to *The Bed?* Framed, it hangs vertically. A stiffened pillow rests on a folded back quilt, to the tiresome geometric pattern of which the lower part of the bed is reduced. The pillow and the pattern are all that remain of reality when the beloved object underwent the Abstract-Expressionist vivisection. . . .

Ever since Barnett Newman presented a plane which could be visualized either as divided from top to bottom by a narrow strip of color, or as the background for a figure represented by the strip, the sign has been menaced by the resurgence of the symbol. One is reminded of Duchamp's challenge to Picasso's, Braque's, and Matisse's continued reproduction of a like image, by introduction of the ready-made into the realm of painting as symbol of the remade. Through their reduction to a single or double line, Newman's painted signs emerge in emblazoned aloneness.

Jasper Johns extinguishes the emblematic character of a given sign, the flag, the target, a set of stencil numbers, the name of a poet of clichés (Tennyson). The target of blue and yellow circles holds the implication that from the marksman's stand it would be seen as a sphere of green. His *Flag* against an orange background leaves the impression of a struggle between the orange and the red in which sight is lost of the blue field. From a national emblem the flag becomes a symbol of ambiguity; from the insignia it is converted into poetry.

Enclosed in boxes over some of the targets, Johns hides the winner's prizes. One set contains the casts of a face painted a hopeless orange, eyes silenced, lips closed. Another set holds the casts of isolated parts of the human body saturated in purple, green, or pink. It amounts to the same: oneness has been killed, whether by the repetition of that face or by the subdivision of that body.

In other versions, the target, the flag, and the numeral have been pitilessly blanched, thereby exposing the encaustic's varied surface. As long as we read according to the letter, a veil is upon our face. Monet

Jasper Johns: *Numbers*, 1964. Sculpmetal on canvas. 14′ x 9′. In the collection of the New York State Theatre, gift of the Albert A. List Foundation. Photograph courtesy of Leo Castelli Gallery, New York.

was the first to lift it by veiling cathedrals. To read according to the spirit we must be in ecstasy; and to read according to the spirit of painting, the artist must displace, for *ec-stasis* means out of place. In a recent logarithmic set of numerals, so blue, so orange, so Bonnard, the squares belonging to a 3 and a 5 have been occupied by paint and paper, by curves and colors and the absent 3 and 5.

If a flashlight instead of a gun is aimed at the target of displaced colors, the silence grows louder. This vessel of light is coated in the dead silver of lead in tribute to those who worship the petrified.

What is the function of a sign that has lost its significance? What can Notre Dame have meant to a fifteenth-century Greek who had fled invaded Constantinople and had lost Hagia Sophia? Of these two cathedrals which is the true one, the Gothic or the Byzantine, the Catholic of *Our Lady* or the Greek of *Holy Wisdom*? Which of these two churches is dedicated to the true Verb? Which contains the heretical, the out-of-place, message?

CALIGULA*

He that speaketh his own speaketh a lie. (John 8:44)

The lie is a private affair, and by turning a fire in Rome into his own private fire Nero demonstrated to the world at large how important it was for him to be a liar. Contrary to this emperor, a victim of imperial tyranny, the Apostle John, from his forced residence in Patmos, viewing the flames of a sea-born volcano embracing the heavens, in majestic sentences explained to seven churches the true meaning of fire. For that which is our own to cease to be a lie others must accept it. (This does not mean that John would agree to this interpretation of Truth!) It is a wise ruler to whose fortunes his subjects are bound. He is the opposite of Timon of Athens who learned at his expense that giving is not binding. Is not giving a private affair? The Apostle John's great achievement was to bind men to truth by arousing their fear. *Religion* evokes *religare* (to bind): "Much do move me the *amor et timor* [love and fear] of God. Fear because He is just, love because He is merciful."[1] For the Christian the ungodly is a fool, for, according to King David, *"The fool hath said in his heart, There is no God."*[2] Unbelief leads to lawlessness, as Dostoevski

---

* Reprinted from *Art News*, November, 1959.
[1] Augustinus, *Exposition of the Book of Psalms*, Psalm 71, Sermon 1:1.
[2] Psalm 14:1.

had prophesied, elaborating on a Socratic theme. Unlike him, the dedicated revolutionist overthrows a given set of rules to establish another. But the island tyrant, a Trujillo of Plato's Sicily or a caesar of Russia, by turning the council of the wise into a circus, rules through folly. The archetype of the fool as ruler is Caligula, who had the insight to realize that *Homo sapiens* is fascinated by folly. Caligula seduced his subjects by his transgressions. Excited by arbitrariness, the avid masses ask, "What next?"

Significantly in the greatest of all stories of seduction, the seducer is a creeping thing, a serpent, for seduction is below where truth is to be found; it is far from the word that is in the beginning. The philosophic counterpart of the ungodly fool is the cynic who substitutes dog for God as criterion of truth. Thanks to the cynic, what had been considered as lawlessness became an antilogos—the spirit of contradiction: *antilogia.*

In our time the cynic's position was taken over by the Surrealists, who represent contradiction in terms of a logos emanating from the unconscious that floods our dreams with lawless actions. With Surrealism, *antilogia,* identified with irrationality, is metamorphosed into doubt. Doubt is that no-man's-land set between lie and truth where folly wanders. The fool is now he who, like Rimbaud, says in his heart, "Je est un autre." Doubt is as old as poetry. In the psalms, where faith is so eloquently proclaimed, doubt is movingly touched upon by David whenever he no longer knows if death is nothing more than sleep; doubt creeps into the passages of the Apocalypse in which silence bids us to *not know* whether resurrection is an awakening from unbelief or from death, whether the millennium is in the music of the spheres or in the water of the fountain.

The fool's power of seduction is in his make-believe participation in our activity which he in fact interrupts for the sake of an interlude of fiction. Caligula reversed the process by tempting his subjects to interrupt their occupations to assume a role in his reality.

The penalty of succumbing to seduction is death, as Adam and Eve were taught. Breathlessly the crowd in the circus waits for the tightrope acrobat to falter. This seducer meets the challenge by undertaking the vertiginous. He assumes a narcissistic role to fascinate those for whom his power of seduction is a temptation. Unlike the king's gestures the seducer's actions have to be vertiginous, "and what have kings that privates have not too, save ceremony?"

Ceremonies are performances unfolded slowly so that nothing can be omitted or missed; the vertiginous act is executed so swiftly that one hardly knows how it was done. Ceremony is the apotheosis of Order. Since 1914, when the world re-entered a Time of Trouble, ceremony has lost prestige. All the great men of action of the new era appear vertiginous: Lenin and Trotsky, Mussolini and Hitler. Vertiginous, too, is the feat accomplished by the hero of the inter-bellum period, Charles Lindbergh.

But in an age of anxiety, when the destiny of disenchanted people is placed in the hands of prosaic rulers, vertiginous performances can no longer be executed in the world of reality. As early as the time of the Spanish Civil War, Dali undertook to transform the upsetting Surrealist irrationality into pure nonsense, and became a court jester. Seduction, however, has the forbidden for its prerequisite, and Dali, so gifted with hindsight (as is suggested by his posterior view of Gala looking at herself in a mirrorless reflection), is an authentic false Vermeer. The virtuoso into which Dali had metamorphosed himself requires the repetition of a past performance. The acclaim received by the virtuoso is an acknowledgment that his repetition is perfect. Through perfection the artist will shed the poet's otherness to become the egoist who says "I am that I am."

The virtuoso is a castrated seducer. Unable to tempt, he fascinates by his ability to avoid mistakes. He inebriates us with abstinence. For a poet what could be more frustrating than to be unable to seduce? Yet this would be his fate if he were reduced to silence by having his doubts sucked into oblivion. But I am anticipating. Ever since the artist entered Cézanne's gardens, he knew he would be offering unappetizing apples. In van Gogh's whirlwinds there is no trace of insanity, and his vision is as clear as John's in the Apocalypse. But for a seer, madness begins from the moment he is met with silence, for how else is he to know if what he says is not a lie? If he is not, as Nero was, a fake, who is there to dissuade him from the temptation of silencing his voice for ever? But self-slaughter is a trap; by leaving speech in suspense a void is created where a poet stood. The void that the dancer on the tightrope avoids! By creating a gap the *heauton timoroumenos* of Baudelaire casts the shadow of doubt upon the brightness of virtuosity. Through the invocation of what remained uncommunicated, suicide violates speech. The soft breath that passed over Modigliani's faces is now nothing more than a tender coat of paint on a savage mask. Maiakovski's roaring images are but toys of a titanic soul unable to hurl rocks at tyrants.

Unlike Maiakovski's heroic despair, René Crevel's allegiance, divided between Surrealism and Communism, led him finally to end his own life as his faint-hearted hero had done in a novel, significantly called *La Mort difficile*. Was it out of faintheartedness, too, that a friend and admirer of Crevel, the disillusioned Klaus Mann, killed himself? But escape from doubt through death is antipoetic, as, to cease doubting, is to fear inspiration.

Arshile Gorky, on the contrary, was unable to escape

from suicide. Feeling that silence was closing upon him from all sides, he came to doubt that he could ever communicate, as is suggested by those ropes he left hanging from trees, with the emptiness of despair, abdicating as it were in favor of another. He moved from branch to branch toward death as he had moved from bough to bough in quest of tortured forms that were to give life to his sinuous lines.

No modern suicide can compare in grandeur to that of the cynic Peregrinus who immolated himself on the funeral pyre at the Olympic games of A.D. 165 in the presence of the emperor. Fusing suicide with sacrifice, Peregrinus desecrated ceremony.

When order is neither embellished by ceremony nor threatened by revolt, taste is at the mercy of frivolity.

Today we are swept once more by a wave of romanticism and bathed in a tempest of asymmetry which the timorous would like to contain in a pool of colors, for great is their fear that our precarious balance could be endangered by sibylline words and dissonant voices. No more than the bee whose message is conveyed by a dance is the artist's communication to be limited to an action.

The action that has itself for an end is thinking (as we know since Aristotle), while the action of building a house has an end beyond itself. Those who claim that painting or a certain type of painting can be comprehended in terms of action should recall that interest in thinking cannot be dissociated from the method of thinking, thanks to which conclusions can be verified and calculations rediscovered, as Pascal rediscovered Euclidian theorems. The interest of a painting lies in the uniqueness achieved through an incomplete adherence to a method of painting—of tracing perspective or harmonizing colors. The reasons vary for departing from the road of painting—*methodos* means "with the road." A Renaissance painter wants to adjust purely pictorial calculations to reality represented by figures against a background, while a modern painter, who excludes from his work natural and geometric forms, obtains unique effects by disturbing the course of calculations. No end is reached through the action of painting comparable to the solution arrived at through the process of thinking. Painting remains incomplete so that others might share the artist's doubts and fears. The artist's talent is in his ability to seduce us to share his point of view. Like music, painting can become the expression of perturbations such as shook the soul of King David and the universe of St. John.

Since paintings of the perturbed artists became worth a furtune, painters have been regally treated and forced to live under the curse that *the king can do no wrong.* But like Caligula they are tempted to prove the contrary. More of a lawbreaker than a puppet, the artist will question the validity of moral and aesthetic taboos, posing again and again the seducer's question "Why not?"

If what the artist proposes is never discussed, how is he to know if what he does deserves to be accepted? Wasn't it Picasso's misfortune to have had *Cahiers d'Art* of Zervos for a wastepaper basket? The artist is manipulated by those who to his doubts oppose what is their own: his works. They silence doubt as, interpreted in terms of property, it spells out insecurity. In the privileged position occupied now by the artist recognized as a virtuoso, even suicide becomes meaningless, for as the case of De Staël suggests, it is but another successful gesture or the signal for another to undertake a vertiginous performance. Not being his brother's keeper, J. D. Salinger with impunity transmuted into faultless words the guilt his poet brother had found unbearable. The virtuoso's sole possible sin is to commit the fatal faux pas of the tightrope dancer. His career should end abruptly, for it is in the nature of enchantment to be contained within an interval which detracts attention from work and play, from prayer and sacrifice. The spell of Caligula was brought to an abrupt end when his subjects whom he had turned into his private property ceased to be fascinated. The fool, forever seduced by his own virtuosity, is like the giddy driver who forgets that the machine is more than a piece of property and that by following its movement it can kill him.

How deafening is the ensuing silence! The private life of a public figure has come to an end. It is said that poets laid wreaths every year on Nero's tomb; it is said that beatniks sleep with earphones plugged to noise boxes so as to detect the motion of sound. Instead of Dostoevsky's sound of action, all that reaches us is noise. For poets who color words or canvas not to be choked by their own verbosity there is a magic filter, but the diviners who know how to make sound pulsate with silence are few. It is said that when Heraclitus was asked to explain action to a group of wise men, he raised his finger several times, and then departed.

THE COBBLER AND THE GAMBLER*

Freud once said to Dali that, when looking at a Surrealist painting, instead of asking himself what was its unconscious meaning, he asks what is its conscious meaning. Implicit in Freud's remark is the charge that Surrealism had not understood that art is a sublimated form of unconscious desires.

Surrealism made us aware that since Freud internalized tragedy we have become too self-conscious to identify ourselves with actors assuming the role of a Jocasta or a Hamlet. Freud's interpretation of catharsis calls for a post-Aristotelian interpretation of art as sublimation.

Aristotle invalidated Plato's doctrine which condemned painting for imitating reality; Aristotle claimed that imitation performs a salutary psychological function which he called "catharsis." If Surrealism reflects our unconscious, must it be dismissed for not being able to produce anything better than a false reality, comparable to the illusory reality we see in a mirror? According to Plato the only true makers are, in the first place, God, viewed as the creator of ideal forms, and then the craftsmen who realize ideal form by making such objects as shoes and beds.

For the magician who invokes images, the Greeks substituted the craftsman who imitates nature. The former, by attributing power to chosen objects was either himself deceived or deceived others. The crea-

* Reprinted from *Art News*, Summer, 1962.

tion of the illusion of reality corresponds less to a desire to lead others into error—as Plato feared—than to the urge to communicate an experience to one's neighbors. Since it has been observed that when dreaming in sleep the eyes move to follow images, Susanne Langer's theory that only man can see images became invalid. Yet, the capacity to reproduce images is undoubtedly a human prerogative. Unlike dreams and magic, whose powers derive from an inability to distinguish between illusion and reality, between the sign and what is signified, the painter's talent lies in his ability to express himself through images. By means of graphic expression the image is both isolated from the boundlessness of physical reality and salvaged from flowing into oblivion with the dream. Since Impressionism, however, we no longer view appearances as necessarily corresponding to reality. Having learned that parallels meet, we do not expect the artist to imitate a reality which is as deceptive as a mirror. Modern painting gradually gave up copying in order to interpret. This is true of painters as dissimilar as Monet and Magritte. When in his *Red Model*, Magritte fuses the shoe with the foot, the inner with the outer, he is no more photographing a dream than Monet is registering reality in his presentation of cathedrals. With Magritte dreams and reality are as two parallels that have reached the point where they meet. It is not in Surrealism but in medieval or ancient works that we find imitation of a fantastic reality inhabited by centaurs, cockatrices, and dragons.

What is the prototype of Magritte's shoes? This is not a question some are likely to ask when seeking out the mystery of Jan van Eyck's Arnolfini Wedding portrait. It is the incongruous details that suggest hidden meanings in this ostensibly official portrait; we are mystified by the patterns placed in the very foreground, the position of the wife before the conjugal bed who thus finds herself on her husband's left, the joining of hands under a mirror in which the couple's backs are reflected and which is surmounted by the painter's signature. For Plato imitation is deceit, but a Flemish Apelles may have wished to insinuate that appearance conceals a secret meaning. The solution of enigmas lies in the future, which, according to the Ancients, cannot be seen because it is back of us.

Unlike great works of the past whose subject matter presents often enough tough iconological problems, modern painting gives rise to phenomenological ones. In classic art representation and interpretation can be treated separately; in modern works they become indistinguishable aspects of the very process of painting. While we do not need to grasp van Eyck's meaning to enjoy his imitation of reality, we do have to decipher a Cubist painting before we can see what it imitates.

Theories of imitation assume that the artist is a maker, a *poietes* (poet). *Making* presupposes the existence of a place in space that can be filled with made things, be it shoe, bed, or mirror. Aesthetics, when comprehended in relation to *making*, are concerned with knowing how to fill a space without either overcrowding or leaving it too bare. This happy medium will be achieved through awareness of the discontinuity between a given space and its objects. Modern art has, however, trained us to look with suspicion at this discontinuity that tends to form a gap that makes the space surrounding a figure look awkward and hollow. To overcome this defect the artist must reduce figure and space to a common denominator consisting of line and color. Instead of imitating reality the artist translates it into a pictorial language.

The gaps and hollows seen by Fauves and Cubists in classic painting, the Surrealists find, as it were, in the discontinuity between dream and reality.

Mastering discontinuity, Magritte reduces the inner and outer world to a common denominator: illusion.

When he converts a rock into the likeness of a sculptured garment, a vessel emptied of the human being, he is treating the images in strictly pictorial terms: the implication being that his image is a double of one not to be found in reality, either physical or fictitious. Magritte convinces because he has found the scale that enables the viewer to differentiate among the landscape, his mental image of it, and the painted replica.

Manifestly, when the artist is no longer, or only secondarily, preoccupied with imitation of a given reality, whether natural, infernal, or ideal, he no longer can be compared to a maker of objects. Without imitation there can be no catharsis. Freud, no admirer of modern art, questioned the conscious meaning of a Surrealist painting, inviting the comparison of artists such as Dali and Magritte to unscrupulous cobblers, makers of poor shoes. However, there is no difference between Freud's criticism of Surrealism and that of abstract art by those who, sneeringly, ask when looking at a Gorky or a Pollock, "What does it mean?"

The artist is no longer obliged to imitate reality as Apelles was to listen to a cobbler when the latter pointed out a mistake in the depiction of a shoe. Since process has become part of the content of painting, pedantic critics would do well to remember the answer given by Apelles to the cobbler when he ventured to proffer his opinion on more than the shoe: "Sutor ne super crepidam" ("Cobbler, do not rise above the shoe," according to Pliny).

If, like a machine, a painting were the product of a blueprint, it could be remade. But what we appreciate in a work of art is a uniqueness so complete that the artist himself may not remake the same picture. Besides, there are no more formulas for producing masterpieces than there are for winning at roulette.

It was in the name of chance that the Epicureans challenged the belief in the world as a work of a

Maker. Yet this doctrine was so contrary to the common way of thinking that Cicero dismissed it lightly by remarking that four hundred successive Venus throws (the lucky number in the Roman game of dice) was enough to prove that such a remarkable performance could be achieved only through God's will.

In the work of painters who do not imitate makers, chance becomes an indispensable element of the composition. It is introduced either through a lapsus, a slip of the hand, or by accident. Chance is invoked by loosening control over material: letting the paint drip or spread, painting with uninhibited gestures of arm and body; even the reaction of color upon color has recently been left to chance. As in patternless abstractions the effect on the canvas of an additional patch of color is unpredictable, and composition becomes an experiment. Unlike the scientist who must be in control of every element of his experiment so that it can be repeated, the artist engages himself in his experiment so that it could never be repeated. To enjoy this type of painting, we no more need to know why the yellow de Kooning placed next to a blue recedes or advances, than we need to know how van Eyck managed to create the sense of depth in the Arnolfini portrait. In each case the painting comes to life.

There is magic in the looking glass's power to efface images, as is implied in the myth of Perseus gazing into the mirror while he murdered Medusa. Abstract art with its indeterminate forms invites the beholder to enter the picture mentally, the way we bodily enter the mirror, to complete the painting in our mind's eye. By stressing discontinuity of rhythm, Action Painting forces awareness of the threatening presence of interruptions, reawakening in our unconscious fears that arise whenever the heart misses a beat.

Magic is shrouded in mystery; like virility, it can be lost. The further man increases his power over his environment, the more imperative it becomes to invoke magic. Awareness of mystery operates as a safety valve against the omnipresent fear of the unconquerable: death. In mystery doubt is cultivated. To doubt is a sign of maturity, for it is an evidence that the new will not be rejected in the name of authority. It is the child who needs reassurance that he is not fatherless. For having said, "One thing I know, that I know nothing," Socrates was accused of introducing new gods. It is in the language of doubt that the artist expresses himself when he remains in touch with his anxiety. After all, it may never be given to him to cast again the Venus throw.

II.
FOCUS
ON
POP

WHY NOT POP ART?*

In the course of conversation on the subject of Pop Art, a young artist was asked about *I Love You with My Ford,* a painting in which Rosenquist juxtaposes the front bumper of a Ford, the still profile of a prone girl, and spaghetti-like tomato-red coils—the total suggesting a highway accident with the coils substituting for spilled intestines. The retort was that had Rosenquist wished to show intestines, he would have painted just that. Spaghetti is spaghetti is spaghetti! And did not T. S. Eliot claim that the spirit killeth but the letter keepeth alive? Another aspect was demonstrated by Rauschenberg when he replied to a suggestion that he paint a portrait of Iris Clert by cabling her: "This is a portrait of Iris Clert if I say so."

For He spake and it was done sounds forceful, but is it convincing since we know it to be an assumption based on an inability to distinguish the word from the act? When in the *Key of Dreams* (1930) Magritte combines images with irrelevant words, the egg with the word "acacia," the bowler hat with the word "snow," an empty glass with the word "tempest," he re-presents objects by signs rather than by images. What Magritte did *not* do was to confuse the sign with the signified.

Jim Dine in his series of paintings of tools combines the images of hammers with real hammers which then become unreal because they are deprived of their

* Reprinted from *Art and Literature,* Spring, 1965.

James Rosenquist: *I Love You with My Ford,* 1961. Oil on canvas. 84¼" x 95⅝" (two panels). In the collection of the Moderna Museet, Stockholm. Photograph courtesy of Leo Castelli Gallery, New York.

utility by being included in a useless object, that is, a painting. Still more radical, however, had been the attitude of Duchamp when he introduced a bottle dryer into an art exhibit. George Brecht manages to break down further the distinction utilitarian-aesthetic by obliging us to view a combination of objects solely as an event. In an "event" in which a stool is placed on a rug, a ball of wool on the stool, and a red ball on the rug next to the stool, it is enough to remove the red ball for this event to be superseded.

Pop Art is the complementary opposite of Surrealism. When confronted with the juxtaposition of an umbrella and a sewing machine, we ask "Is it art?" because of the difficulty of adjusting ourselves to a situation which appears too incongruous to be subjected to an aesthetic order. When viewing a flashlight painted flat-gray by Jasper Johns, we ask "Is it art?" because of our difficulty in perceiving the difference between this image and a real flashlight. When George Brecht speaks of events, he is trying to narrow further the difference between art and reality.

To return to our starting point: It would hardly be tolerated if a reporter in his account of a violent death mentioned disemboweled intestines next to the victim's body when in fact spaghetti-in-tomato-sauce was spilled alongside. However, if a patient recounts to his analyst a dream of an accident in which he saw reddish spaghetti next to the victim's body, the doctor might well suspect that the spaghetti stood for intestines. The new school in literature and painting demands from us the rejection of all association of one image with another in the name of reality. To psychological insight it opposes factual observation; believing that pleasure is to be derived from the flat statement and not from ambiguous meanings, it encourages exploration of everyday reality and not the fantastic realm which the Surrealists made their own. Literal-mindedness as criterion demonstrates that

Rosenquist is not a good example of the Pop artist: a recent painting, *The Early Morning*, patently invites us to associate images with objects not represented. Rosenquist places in the center of the canvas a huge oval which in the upper or sky section is shown merely in outline but in the lower section becomes a sliced orange. The title of the painting prompts us to view the sun-kissed orange as a substitute for the sun.

Unlike Rosenquist, Jasper Johns cannot be accused of erring in the direction of the melodramatic. Johns' image is the antithesis of a double image: it demands that we see it as a variant of the prototype. Had he changed the composition of the flag by placing the stars parallel to the stripes, would such a painting retain the impact of the gray monochrome version? It is to be doubted, for the affinity between the painted version and the original would be too indistinct. What is so often appealing in a friend's child is its likeness to its parent.

If we accepted the thesis that the spirit killeth and the letter keepeth alive, we would be unable to say of a kouros represented with one foot forward that it denotes a man walking because to stand with one leg before the other is not a proof that one is not standing still. Does this imply that representation of movement in a work of sculpture necessitates turning it into a mobile, as with Calder, or replacing it with mechanical devices as does Tinguely? Was it not the great achievement of Picasso in *Guernica* to suggest movement by a process of simultaneity that does not involve tricks of three-dimensionality à la Tintoretto? Rauschenberg's recent work permits hope that despite his endorsement of the thesis of literal meaning he will succeed in suggesting motion in terms of the indeterminate pattern introduced by Pollock. But it should be recalled that motion in painting, like silence in music, may be for the artist the kiss of death. What we enjoy in Rauschenberg's paintings in which superimposed images or a succession of images involve repetitions is not the movement but the suggestion of movement. The modern artist avoids imitating the vain deceits of the mirror.

George Segal's plaster casts of humans are more unreal than wax dolls and too real to be taken for works of art; they seem to have been fashioned to fit into non-existent situations. Pop Art is sharpening our sensitivity by emphasizing the objective aspect of being at the expense of the subjective one, creating thereby artificial situations akin to those produced by Giacometti in his group statues or by Robbe-Grillet in his novels. This superobjectivity to which the new realism introduces us does not justify a dissociation of images from ideas as the defenders of a literal interpretation insist. If painters were to treat images as signs the way the mathematician and the composer treat their sets of signs, they would have to standardize images by transforming them into pictographs such as hieroglyphs.

Pop Art focuses on the popular ready-made image. This is undoubtedly a healthy reaction to the cult of the dream image of the interbellum period with its political and sexual wishful thinking by the fellow travelers of Marx and Freud. Pop Art is tailored to the needs of "the lonely crowd" that congregates in subways and fills highways, gazing at ads and billboards with the fascination medieval masses gathered in churches gazed at holy images—icons. Pop Art is the art of making Pop icons in an era when magic has withdrawn from mosaics and stained glass to reappear on the television screen. "I am so mesmerized by television that I want to buy all that it advertises!" a City College student was heard to exclaim. Dada with its ready-mades, Surrealism with its *objets trouvés*, Abstract Expressionism with its emphasis on action, have been resorted to by artists to free us from art. But then comes the critic to prove that what passes for non-art is actually a new form of art. The critic blesses the artist's defiance of art. Thus critics have pointed out that a bottle dryer placed on a mantelpiece requires us to forget its usage and to see it together with the objets d'art in the room. Likewise a weirdly shaped stone is promoted to the rank of a work of art in a setting which includes works by Tanguy or Miró. A painting resulting from an artist's gesticulation appeals to our understanding of the elements which make it different from familiar compositions.

From *Le Déjeuner sur l'Herbe* to *Martinson's Coffee* by Warhol, the question is repeatedly asked, "Is this art?" Modern art is a cultural phenomenon corresponding to the thinking of man of the non-Euclidean age: *Why not* assume that parallels meet in the infinity? In the name of this *why not* so eloquently defended by Gaston Bachelard in his *Nouvel Esprit Scientifique*, why not detach forms and colors from objects, and combine them in a new pattern? . . . Why not make the pattern indeterminate? . . . Why not increase the probability of obtaining an unexpected result by including chance among the elements of our calculation? Pop Art rests on the assumption that man is no longer a child of nature but of the machine. Warhol may be the purest of Art-Popists when he says: "The things I want to show are mechanical. Machines have less problems. I'd like to be a machine, wouldn't you?"

In fighting for their place in the galleries of Madison Avenue, the brightest of the younger New York artists were impelled to reverse the position of their elders: While Abstract Expressionists reduced to a minimum the difference between creator and creation, Pop Art offered the reduction to a minimum of the difference between the ready-made and the handmade. When Warhol stencils by silk-screen process his rows of Marilyn Monroe, one is reminded of sheets of stamps. But unlike the philatelist who will scrutinize a sheet in the hope of discovering an imperfection, the critic is interested in seeing how in his successive renditions an artist can avoid producing differences when he touches in the colors. When Bob Watts, improving on Warhol, makes real stamps of his miniature Pop images, he is, as it were, challenging us to look for machine-made improvements on his handmade originals.

The New Realism viewed as the imitator of machine-made images marks the triumph of abstract art. It is not the historical or the psychological or the sociological or the political aspect of iconology that requires our attention, but only the phenomenological use of banal images. Bob Watts' sheets of "stamps" belong with the compositions of La Monte Young which demand that the listener attune himself to variations in the lengths of silences falling between a series of repeated notes struck over and over by the pianist's elbows.

Repetition is the motif of D'Arcangelo's painting series: inspired by a cinematic view of images he succeeds by means of slight changes in the highway-scape to give an awareness of roadwise progression of time. In the artificial world of Pop Art how are we to measure differences? Perhaps Bob Morris gives the answer with his three twelve-inch flat-gray yardsticks of slightly differing lengths, for it is our inability to distinguish the correct measure from the false one that stirs our sensibility. Is this not a post-Euclidian way of representing the Sphinx's enigma? Deprived of his measuring rods, man would be obliged to return to a pre-Euclidian concept of life, unable to oppose the order of reason to chance's disorder. We should never confuse the inclusion of chance in an orderly sequence with the absence of order. In the first instance chance makes its presence felt in terms of interruption, while in the second instance chance cannot be distinguished from formlessness. But were we to interpret interruption literally, we would have to view it—no more, no less—as an obstacle in the path of movement. Hence when the work of art is conceived merely as process (theory of action painting), interruptions of the process are nothing more than happenings. This is equally true of advertisement when it is dissociated from the commodity it is meant to advertise. Ads become happenings that distract our attention when walking or riding, when reading or talking.

When we narrow our view of the world to the point at which all events are reduced to happenings, changes become meaningless since they no longer are seen in historical perspective. This is precisely what John Cage wants the artist to forego. According to Cage, in order to create a purely objective music the composer has to free himself from the impact that time has upon memory and imagination. To the relevance of time Cage opposes that of chance. In a recent essay, "The End of the Renaissance?"[1] Leonard Meyer, comparing Cage's experiments with those of Rauschenberg in painting and Robbe-Grillet in fiction, calls these artists radical empiricists because they substitute chance for causal relations. Empiricism in science and philosophy is undoubtedly literal-minded when *tautological statements* are made of the type A is A. It is doubtful whether Meyer's radical empiricists do likewise, or can be held to do so. When their forerunner, Marcel Duchamp, introduced a urinal into an art exhibition, he made a *synthetic statement*, that is, that our conception of art should be extended to include ready-made objects beside the handmade ones usually seen in art exhibitions; when Rauschenberg claims that a canvas is never empty, he is treating an unpainted canvas in terms of the fullness of a painted one. Furthermore, whenever an artist includes in his paintings effects dictated by irregularities in his canvas or other such accidents, he is making a synthetic state-

[1] *Hudson Review*, Summer, 1963.

ment on the relation of random effect upon his work.

Meyer holds that radical empiricism has abolished communication and produced a nonteleological art. Yet a more rigorous analysis of the works themselves shows, to the contrary, that the above-mentioned artists, as well as their followers, have an end in view clearly in mind, since they make of interruptions in a work in progress and of unforeseen changes in form the prerequisite of their compositions. With these artists, the effects of chance upon form, rather than those of work upon form, becomes the basic aesthetic criterion.

This new art movement actually broadens the scope of the indeterminate pattern introduced by the Abstract Expressionists. Whatever the effects of chance happenings, a work of art, in the last analysis, will always be a synthesis of antithetic parts. Its aesthetic interest lies in a pattern that a viewer consciously or unconsciously associates with previous experiences. Consciousness functions in a historical context formed by the world of experience, which is why the meaning of synthetic statements cannot be exhausted by a literal interpretation.

When the composition includes a multiplicity of figures, as is often the case in the works of Rauschenberg, what we respond to is not the presence of *unaccountable* happenings, but the *variety* of unexplained episodes. Reacting to the systematization of a mechanized world, Robert Rauschenberg has rediscovered—via the comics—the pleasures of the "string of events" technique of the pre–Renaissance, however different the intent. Obviously enough, the present-day artist finds his source of inspiration in the layout of newspapers and picture magazines rather than in the illuminated Psalters and Books of Hours. Like Warhol, Rauschenberg is a child of the machine; but rather than imitate industry's shallow successes, he creates an assemblage of images worthy of the great painters of hells and earthly paradises.

POP ICONS*

Since modern art became the art of the Establishment, its opponent has been anti-art. The dispute between the champions of art and the sponsors of anti-art brings to mind the famous eighteenth-century quarrel between the proponents of the art of the ancients, in the name of perfection, and those of the moderns, in the name of progress. Today, modern art is viewed in terms of art history, and anti-art in terms of "life."

During the 1920's, Surrealism was Cubism's anti-art, as Pop Art is the anti-art of Expressionism. In the 1937 *Portrait of a Lady*, Picasso reinterpreted Cubist multiple planes in psychological terms, suggesting split personality by fusing the side and front view of a face into one; the second eye is between two noses, or the two eyes are shown frontally and the single nose in profile.[1] The distance between his Cubist *Fernande* and his Surrealist Dora Maar might be measured in terms of the distance betwen Apollinaire and André Breton.

During this, the seventh decade of our century, doctors of philosophy would prefer to "pre-empty" Pop

* Reprinted from *Pop Art*, ed. Lucy R. Lippard, New York: Frederick A. Praeger, 1966.

[1] See Alfred H. Barr, Jr., *Picasso: Fifty Years of His Art* (New York: Museum of Modern Art, 1946), p. 209; also *Portrait* (1938), p. 215. I believe both to be portraits of Dora Maar.

Art of anti-art. Study of paintings in terms of basic patterns zeroes the difference between Roy Lichtenstein and Nicholas Krushenick; concentrically zeroes that between Jasper Johns and Kenneth Noland; squares that between Andy Warhol's bouquets and Josef Albers' rectangles. If form is the basic criterion for judging art, then why not also compare a basic pattern of two different paintings to analogous patterns found in nature? Why not compare the dots of a Lichtenstein to the spots of a ladybird, and Poons' dots to the dots of that other insect, known to the uninitiated in entomological classifications as a false ladybird? Don't let us *pointilliste* our eyes! The integration of anti-art into art is undoubtedly a valid preoccupation, allowing the erection of partitions. What would museums do without walls? If the critic's role is to establish that anti-art is art, perhaps a sibyl will prophesy the coming of anti-critics.

Let us enjoy images as images, as we enjoy games for the sake of playing. Addiction to images is a dream derivative. To be communicated in visual terms, sights seen, whether in sleep or in the world around us, must be given form in a selected medium. Since a reproduction is not intended to be confused with its original, the artist in his painting will include only those aspects of the beheld which he either wishes to or is able to reproduce. Pictures of reality or of dreams that have crucial cultural impact are icons. In our century the first great icons are Cubist. Thus, in his post-Euclidian vision, Picasso projected on a single plane a synthetic view of the multiple planes of a man playing the violin.

From the Book of Daniel and from our dreams, we have learned that the key images are those of people and places. Portraits and landscapes are the bread and wine of painting. Let them be nourishing and appetizing, fermented and stimulating! The early Cubist paintings are exquisite. The guitar, the bottle of wine,

Roy Lichtenstein: *Temple of Apollo,* 1964. Oil and magna on canvas. 94" x 128". In the collection of Mr. and Mrs. Robert Rowan. Photograph courtesy of Leo Castelli Gallery, New York.

the *journal*, the stilled cinematic descent provide glimpses of those non-Dutch interiors where the sophisticated bourgeois speculated on Bergson, Apollinaire, and Jaurès. The Cubist's dissection of form corresponds to the socialist's critique of institutions and to the psychologist's analysis of man. Cubism endowed us with a post-Ptolemaic "Fayum" image of man (a preview of Byzantine icons), but not with a post-Copernican view of the world. The Industrial Revolution outspeeded clocks, but the Futurist's view of the phenomenon remained trivial, and was exploded by De Chirico in the name of anxiety. Moreover, with De Chirico's biscuits, matchboxes, and fish molds, anti-art elements were introduced into modern art. From his *Gare Montparnasse* back to Palladio, through a metaphysical reality, a world of false dreams is unraveled. Anxiety is indirectly derived from the Greek word *gonia* (corner). De Chirico, Ernst, Magritte, Tanguy are concerned. What relics are to worshippers of icons, Dada and Surrealist objects are to the devotees of modern icons, that is, things that possess an element of magic, of having been made without hands, as Marcel Duchamp's term "ready-made" implies; of having been assembled by a mysterious force—the Surrealist found object.

Difficulty of legibility is what Cubism and Surrealism have in common; Cubist statements are not clear; Surrealist meanings are obscure. Matisse and Léger are undoubtedly the twentieth century's great masters of clarity, and their influence today on both Pop and Abstract artists is indisputable. Their ability to simplify is admirable, but I object to the casual manner in which they treat their subject matter. Are Matisse's odalisques pure imitations of Persian women, or are they *Vogue* imitations of French women? Are Léger's workers militant members of the proletariat or performers of a *ballet mécanique*? This weakness of

Matisse becomes glaring when we look at Wesselmann's *Great American Nudes*—prototypes of America seen through the mass media. The weakness of
Léger becomes obvious when the paintings are re-
examined through the middle-class character of
Léger's proletarianism. Pop artists, by forgetting even
the immediate past, focus their attention on the
"positivism" of the present.

After the fermented light of the Impressionists, the
aromatic pines and apples of Cézanne, the intoxicating
colors of the Fauves, the alcohol of dreams of the Surrealists, defeated Paris was reduced to the imageless
insomnia of Existentialism. The center of art moved
to New York. With the self-assurance of Periclean
Athens, New York mixed its Doric and Ionic elements.
American Abstract Expressionism detached automa-
tism from the Surrealists' imagistic painting and, in so
doing, liberated abstract art from its obsession with
geometric form. Now we can make and appreciate
the distinction between automatic abstraction and calculated abstraction. Historically, abstract art has its
roots in Protestant and Judaic iconoclasm. It should
be born in mind that France is the only great power
in Europe that, owing to the atheist spirit of the
Revolution of 1789, passed from the medieval Catholic religion to the modern world without going through
the iconoclastic phase of Protestantism. In France all
the great movements of modern art, from Impressionism to Surrealism, experimented with images. Max
Ernst, the most important German Surrealist painter,
comes from a Catholic family. In England and in the
United States, two countries with a Protestant culture,
the current battle for the image is waged on behalf of
a previously scorned image, the popular advertisement
of consumer goods. The lowly ad is easily viewed as
anti-art. An orthodox Surrealist sees no virtue in its
use since the ad lacks reference to the esoteric. Surrealism opposes the dream to daydreaming and the

Tom Wesselmann: *Great American Nude # 81*, 1966.
Acrylic on canvas. 53″ x 66″. Photograph courtesy of Sidney Janis Gallery, New York.

myth to reality. Furthermore, emphasis on consumer goods is offensive to the Surrealist on ideological grounds, for he rates production over consumption. Iconoclasm explains why many abstract artists are more shocked by Pop artists' profanation of images than angered by their rejection of abstract art.

Lichtenstein, Wesselmann, and Warhol are no more Pop artists in the original British sense of the term than were Duchamp or Léger Futurists in the Italian sense. If the Italian Futurists had a Vulcan complex, the British Pop artists can be said to have a cornucopia complex, that is to say, a love-hate attitude toward America's wealth as they envisage it through the glossy American magazines.[2] In New York, ready-made vernacular images were first convincingly introduced into works of art by two former Abstract Expressionists, Larry Rivers and Robert Rauschenberg. Followed by Jasper Johns, Jim Dine, and Claes Oldenburg, these artists disfigure the ready-made image to adapt it to an overall indeterminate pattern. Lichtenstein, Wesselmann, Warhol, and D'Arcangelo interpret the ready-made image in terms of calculated abstraction. With the former, the process of making is frequently interrupted by accidents, and with the latter, the formation of images conforms to a definite pattern.

In terms of significance these tendencies are complementary. We would be like the naïve Pre-Raphaelites looking at Botticelli without remembering Piero della Francesca if we included in our collection of icons Lichtenstein but not Rauschenberg, Rosenquist but not Rivers, Wesselmann but not Katz. But D'Arcangelo belongs, and Fairfield Porter does not. By this, I do not mean that the aesthetic contradictions of our time have to be resolved in terms of the humanist's concepts of beauty and truth. The con-

[2] See Jasia Reichardt, "Pop Art and After," *Art International*, Vol. 8, No. 2, February, 1963.

temporary imagists are searching for ways of assimilating a pictorial experience embracing the miniature comic strips and the giant billboards. The illustrated weeklies demonstrate that the reproduction of *The Syndics* by Rembrandt can double as the trademark of Dutch Masters cigars. Why not also include a third version—Larry Rivers' painting of the Dutch Masters ad? Is a ruined Greek temple a historical monument or a TWA ad? What if it turned out to be a Lichtenstein?

Reproduction of the masterpiece refers to an object that is priceless because it is evaluated in historical terms, while the advertisement employing the historical piece refers to a commodity—a pack of cigars or an airplane ticket. Unlike the reproduction of the masterpiece that is meant to evoke the past, the ad encourages us to forget the past by inviting us to satisfy transient urges, to smoke or to travel; the picture of a 1966 Chevy makes us forget the 1965 Chevy; the beauteous Miss Rheingold distracts us from the home where beer is drunk without her. Surrealism sought to overcome the contradiction between desire and reality on the plane of a super-reality. Pop Art deals with a reality that is apt to be the printed reproduction of an image. However, the identification of the reproduction with its model is blocked when we realize (with the help of a magnifying glass) that the image dissolves into the pattern of the grind formed by the benday dots. The grid's network is the threshold on which the reproduction and the printing process meet on an anti-image level. When Lichtenstein focuses on this threshold he forcefully dissociates his blown-up view from the comic-book universe. Jasper Johns achieved similar effects in the mid-1950's when he fused the design of the Star-Spangled Banner with the brushstroke patterns of the encaustic surface. Pop Art can be anti-Pop. Dissociations permit one to dismiss and, eventually, to forget the original. In their time, Surrealists such as Magritte, Tanguy, and Ernst reawakened buried instances of a personal past, and evoked that which is most difficult to remember: the dream, wherein the past is represented under a disguise or mask. But Lichtenstein and Johns chose to veil appearances more lightly by simple technique—grid or encaustic—which add an element of the unexpected without hiding identity. While the Surrealists' effects presented enigmas and masked faces, the effects of the younger men can be best likened to the recognition of a face despite unaccustomed sunglasses—as in Alex Katz's *Ada with Glasses*. With Rauschenberg, Rivers, and their kin, the procedure varies in that they resort to disfiguring the image with brushstrokes and drippings. Either method aims ultimately at personalizing the image.

Lichtenstein has been criticized for his false madonnas. Similar objections could be raised against Wesselmann for degrading the nude, against D'Arcangelo for counterfeiting the road to Bethlehem, against Rosenquist for crashing sacrifices on the road,[3] against Warhol for his hot-selling sepulchral flowers. Art is not a tranquilizer. "Pop Art looks out into the world," says Lichtenstein. The Pop artists look out on the world through reproductions. They paint it the way the Surrealists painted the dream—photographically. Having rejected the role of spiritual sons to some great master, both the Surrealists and the Pop artists have been viewed as anti-artists. The major difference lies in their attitude. Whereas the Surrealist's is lyrical, that of the Pop artist is cool. Therefore the reaction to the Pop image should be cool. Whether the image is or is not a work of art is a secondary consideration. Does the worshipper of an icon of his patron saint care whether the representation is a masterpiece? The icon is for us, when warm for prayer, when cool for companionship. The same applies to the Pop artist's relics:

[3] See previous essay, "Why Not Pop Art," in this volume.

the dead-as-lead flashlights of Jasper Johns, and the handmade metal chocolates of Robert Watts, subtracted from the superficial world of imitation, occupy a place in a reality from which identity has been excluded. Robert Morris' *Swift Night Ruler* stirs our sensibility through our inability to distinguish the correct measure from the false; Aaron Kuriloff's fuse boxes are set in the twilight zone between function and uselessness. Pop Art discovered the Surrealism of the understatement.

IN QUEST OF FOLLY*

Ever since Moses and Plato condemned the makers of illusions, the artist of the Western world was exposed to the danger of being viewed as a propagator of errors. With the advent of modern art, the artist or poet assumes the role of a prodigal son. Has not modern art been repeatedly condemned both in its beginnings and its successive renewals for repudiating truth and beauty? Modern artists are accused of betraying the canons of beauty much the way the prodigal sons of the Church in the Middle Ages were accused of betraying the Word of God.

The Prodigal Son of the Parable as interpreted by the holy fathers is a personification of David's ungodly fool: "The fool hath said in his heart, There is no God" (Psalm 14). By "fool" St. Augustine meant one who leaves the Father's house for a "Far Country" ruled by Satan; that is, one seduced by false doctrines. The folly of the Prodigal Son consisted in his having used free will to please himself rather than to serve God. Yet, as he was neither moron nor mad, he was capable of repentance and return to the fold.

This medieval view of folly in terms of ungodliness went through a profound change in the fifteenth century, as is attested by the writings of Sebastian Brandt. In his crude stories, much reproduced and illustrated in the days of block books, folly was considered in moralistic terms and identified with the vices. It was left to the humanists to detach folly from religious

* Reprinted from *Art and Literature*, Winter, 1967.

Hieronymous Bosch: *The Prodigal Son.* Photograph courtesy of the Rijksmuseum, Amsterdam.

Jacquemart de Hesdin: *Illustration for Psalm 52:3*—"The fool said in his heart there is no God." From the *Psalter of the Duc de Berry.*

overtones. According to Erwin Panowski, Erasmus condemned folly for negating reason.

Having emancipated reason, Descartes made of doubt and probability valid propositions. Thereafter folly could be linked to either excessive doubt or to extreme improbability. The folly of doubt is personified by Hamlet, while the folly of improbability was expounded with great rigorousness by the Marquis de Sade. In his materialistic Manichaeanism, Sade proposed that to be godlike man must be evil, since the world God is assumed to have created is unjust. Sade, by his merciless criticism of deism paved the way for the fool to re-emerge in the atheistic nineteenth century. He is the fool who to Descartes' "Je pense donc je suis" answers, "Je est un autre" (Rimbaud).

The Far Country for which the prodigal sons of modern art leave home is the world of Gauguin and van Gogh, of Max Ernst and Yves Tanguy, of Rimbaud and Lautréamont, of Apollinaire and André Breton. The author of *Nadja*, following Pascal, interprets behavior in terms of intentions. It should be recalled that Pascal refuted the Jesuit doctrine of "the end justifies the means" on the grounds that man should be judged according to his intentions rather than his actions, since free will has been given to him by God to serve God.

Theories of intentions ultimately justify failure-to-do. In this scientific age depth psychology has evolved a dramatic new view of intentions. But psychotherapeutic approaches resorted to in mending a patient's malfunctioning in society generally rely heavily on the assumption that work is salutory. Fixation on work is a Protestant aberration. If, as Martin Luther thought, we can no more co-operate in our salvation than can an inanimate object; if, as Calvin preached, we are not even able to resist the grace of God, there is nothing to deter us from working for our terrestrial well-being without worrying about eternity. This opportunistic interpretation of the new doctrine served primarily the needs of the hard-working middle class, backbone of the Reformation. In its countermove, Catholicism reacted by claiming that salvation can be attained through works that receive the blessing of the Church—hence the famous formula "the end justifies the means," which met with strong opposition from the Jansenists.

In a postreligious concept of man, the Protestant antithesis between work and salvation was overcome by the Marxists and their interpretation of history in terms of the salvation of the human species through the emancipation of the working class. Christian ethics had so conditioned man to accept punishment for original sin that the Marxists "forgot" that their struggle for abolition of economic privileges implies also the liberation of man from the pain of toil. Alone the utopian socialist Charles Fourier, far back in the 1820's, had the audacity to proclaim "le droit à la paresse." Inspired by this idea, André Breton wrote his magnificent "Ode to Fourier."

As I see it, Surrealism's contribution to the ethical problem consists in adopting a Pascalian attitude in a socialist milieu. Surrealism opposes failure-to-do to work on the strength of a psychoanalytically valid interpretation of intentions. Politically, neither Jansenism nor Surrealism could have much appeal, for a theory of intention serves primarily to justify the needs of those intellectuals, poets, and lovers who avoid "doing" in order to concentrate on "feeling." While great reformers of an established "Church," whether Loyola or Trotsky, view salvation in relation to the doctrine that the end justifies the means, prodigal sons like Pascal and Breton find in failure-to-do the libidinal sources of inspiration.

A poet used to viewing behavior in terms of intentions rather than will is more sensitive to the alternatives of choice than to the obstacles confronting him.

Victor Brauner: *The Surrealist,* 1947. In the collection of
Peggy Guggenheim.

Significantly, the alternatives of choice treated in terms of probability were formulated by Pascal while devising a scheme that could be used by gamblers to divide the stake in an unfinished game. Interest in laws of chance was undoubtedly stimulated in the seventeenth century by a growing preoccupation with speculation. Less than a century later, western Europe was to experience a series of financial crises owing to overconfidence in speculation.

The gambler's fascination with chance is shared by the poet, but the motivation is different. The gambler concentrates on risk when he seeks self-fulfillment in an adventure that can bring him wealth, while the romantic poet seeks self-fulfillment through adventures of the soul that enrich his experience. Self-fulfillment was, however, frowned upon by the middle class; adventurers such as Cesare Borgia and "Coriolanus" were admired as great in evil.

For centuries, only in the art of war—a complementary opposite of both work and failure-to-do— was chance recognized as a decisive factor. "There is no human activity that stands in such constant and universal contact with chance as war does," Clausewitz remarked. Furthermore, Clausewitz's description of military leadership is nothing but an avowed eulogy of risk.

According to bourgeois standards developed and perfected by the Reformation, work remains a virtue as long as it is not contaminated by risk. Only the Protestant God gambles by casting salvation on some and damnation on others. The Protestant conviction that work is a virtue was never seriously questioned by the Marxists. But those who do not consider failure-to-do a disgrace may replace work by play. The Surrealists emphasized this with a vengeance, opposing as they do desire to duty. Their games, mostly invented parlor ones, stress chance at the expense of skill, and uselessness over gain. They in fact despise card-players.

In gambling the emphasis is shifted from repetition of the act of playing to interruption of the series of repetitions through loss of money. By courting chance an unlucky player may lose so much as to be unable to continue playing. Not to be able to experience again the excitement of total loss means that the pleasure of playing has been interrupted by loss. By tempting chance we woo the devil. As Kierkegaard explained in his penetrating analysis of Don Giovanni, it is the devil who makes his presence felt through interruption.

It was to the devil that the Prodigal Son was seen to have fallen victim when he reached the Far Country. The Surrealist is a Prodigal Son who does not come back in repentance because he never wants to stop interrupting.

"Je est un autre"; in the poet's name, that is to say, on behalf of his image-impregnated unconscious, the Surrealist undertook to defend failure-to-do before the court of socialist opinion. Surrealism challenged Marxist iconoclasm rooted in the Protestant hostility toward images and their wealthy possessors, the churches and the nobles.

Those rich in imagination or wealth can best afford to maintain illusions and images. Like the socialist-minded followers of St. Francis, the Surrealists wished images to be enjoyed by all. But when disaster visits the country where images are respected and loved, the adventures of the Prodigal Son are forgotten for the sake of the sufferings of Job.

Surrealism is superseded by Existentialism. Intellectuals have no longer the desire to be entertained by illusion; now they focus on dramatization and impoverishment. Who could have been better equipped to make this reorientation in spiritually humiliated France than Sartre? His Protestant background conditioned him to reject images. Significantly, his first book, *L'Imagination*, was written to refute Bergson's theory of cinematic images in favor of the German theory of imageless thinking. As a Frenchman, Sartre was in a better position than most Protestant theoreticians to explain away images to his compatriots. How this could be done in art is brilliantly demonstrated in his Tantalian analysis of Giacometti's sculpture that he interprets in terms of an identification of the vanishing point with the image: no sooner does one look closely at the image than it dissolves.

The irony of fate was that the socialist Surrealist *poverelli* owed their success to the *nouveaux riches* of World War I who desired to possess themselves of images they admired and ones the masses were not willing even to look at.

We are faced in recent years with a paradoxical situation: While poets, painters, and composers multiply chance effects to increase uncertainty, scientists compile ever more statistical information in order to decrease the uncertainty of their predictions. With computers, scientists have been able to predict the recurrence of numbers in roulette; computers can not only determine the patterns of irregularity due to aleatory effects in the composition of an artist's work but can also produce analogous effects—they are capable of producing random verses. The time is come when the artist who resorts to chance is achieving results more easily obtainable by mechanical means.

Why compete with the machine?

Andy Warhol, the Dali of Pop Art, says he paints the way he does because he wants to imitate the machine: "I feel that whatever I want to do and do machine-like is what I want to do." In the age of the machine he who says Yes to the machine is the opposite of the fool who said No. According to David the fool denied God "in his heart," that is, secretly and, by extension, equivocally. The computer is literal-minded; so is the skilled player. To say No, the fool has to be a poet, one who speaks in his heart, that is, a hermetic language.

AND NOW THE SPHINX*

When asked "Is Pop Art a postwar form of Surrealism?" I beg my interrogator to bear in mind that Surrealism is deeply involved in moral issues, while Pop Art is not. Surrealism is passionate and romantic, while Pop Art is cool and pragmatic. Surrealism developed in the intellectual climate of dialectical interpretations of both society and the psyche. Pop Art grew in an age of logical positivism and empiricism. Surrealism relies on symbolism, Pop Art on literalness.

Instead of Max Ernst's wonderland peopled by fabulous women metamorphosed into hybrid birds, what we are shown today is Lichtenstein's stenographer as a heroine of comic-strip melodrama; Delvaux's somnambulistic sirens are replaced by Wesselmann's bland call girl with the eyeless gaze. Dali wants painting to be appetizing, and Oldenburg offers oversized drugstore hamburgers.

Between Surrealism and Pop Art the avant-garde went through a phase of Existentialism that had a profound influence on some of today's best writers and artists.

1. Surrealism

Surrealism challenges reality in the name of freedom of the individual. Like Pascal, the Surrealists interpret

* Reprinted from *The New Art*, ed. Gregory Battcock, New York: E. P. Dutton, 1966.

this freedom in terms of intentions rather than actions, as do the Jesuits and other adherents to the doctrine of "the end justifies the means." Since the Surrealists are involved with passion, and not with salvation, they interpret intentions in terms of desire rather than in terms of freedom of will.

The ambition of Surrealism was to reinterpret on the poetic level Marx's famous aphorism "We have sufficiently explained the world; it is time to transform it." To the Surrealists this involved overcoming the contradiction reality-dream by creating a super-reality.

To achieve these political and literary goals, sacrifices must be borne. The poet must realize that not all desires are desirable, for the most desirable of all desires is love. Through love, and love only, can we overcome the boundaries of the self and achieve that ecstasy, that state beyond bounds in which the I and the Thou are one. To understand what love is, the Surrealist will refer to the letters of Héloïse and Abélard, to Shakespeare's *Antony and Cleopatra*, to the poetry of St. John of the Cross, to Rousseau's *Nouvelle Héloïse*, to the letters of Napoleon Bonaparte to Josephine. Breton's contribution to the exposition of love is *Nadja*, a novel in which insanity becomes an asset of the poet's beloved. Nadja possesses "la beauté du diable."

Since the insane reject reality—for whatever reason—those who believe in the reality of God justifiably recall David's verse "The fool hath said in his heart, There is no God." When therefore André Breton hails insanity as purity, it is as if he were proclaiming that the poet has the right to be irresponsible. Negation of reality in the name of a poetic dream or a political utopia becomes ludicrous in the age of anxiety. "Forget your dreams and hold your breath" advise Kierkegaard's disciples. To Solomon's passionate *Song of Songs* the humility of Job is opposed by Sartre; to

Rimbaud, Dostoevski; to Lautréamont, Kafka; to *Nadja, La Nausée*; to love, death. Freedom from bondage is reinterpreted in terms of freedom in bondage. Sartre believes man can be saved through self-realization, through the "pour soi." What this means is obscure, since the term implies both the collective "we" and the individual "I."[1]

With their *cri du cœur* in praise of love and folly, revolt and irresponsibility, the Surrealists enter the domain of lyricism. The Existentialists, with their attention focused on extreme situations, espouse tragedy.

2. Pop Art

Unlike the Surrealists, who plunge into their souls, and the Existentialists, who explore extreme situations, Pop artists "look out upon the world" (Lichtenstein), boasting of their detachment. The Pop artists' approach poses a serious question: If new art is no longer the reflection of the unconscious or an expression of emotion, can it claim to be a manifestation of modern art? Is it not modern art's great glory to have substituted "inner truth" for Truth (of perspective or reality)—and the uniqueness of an individual's experience to "knowing how to see?" From Turner to Monet, from van Gogh to Picasso and after, modern art stands or falls according to the answer we give to this question. After Picasso come Pollock and de Kooning, who opened our eyes to the enchantment of indeterminate patterns. (The composer John Cage translated Pollock's findings to indeterminate sequences, opposing thereby the stillness-in-movement to Pollock's motion-in-stillness.) Rauschenberg formed indeterminate sequences of dissociated images into a patternless setting. "Something new (spontaneous,

[1] Herbert Marcuse, "Existentialism: Remarks on J.-P. Sartre's *L'Être et le Néant*," in *Philosophy and Phenomenological Research*, VIII, 3; March, 1948.

'specific') is always a language game," says Wittgenstein. This dictum certainly applies to Jasper Johns, as is made clear by an excerpt from the latter's *Sketch Book Notes*: "Make neg. of part of figure and chair. Fill with these layers—encaustic (flesh?), linen Celastic. One thing made of another. One thing used as another. *An arrogant object.* Something to be folded, or bent, or stretched (SKIN?). Beware of the body and the mind. Avoid a polar situation. Think of the edge of the city and the traffic there" (*Art and Literature*, 4, Paris, 1965).

Thus handled, painting could become but a game. The true artist, however, has a spectator in mind— as Sartre has so convincingly demonstrated—and he seeks to engage this viewer, make him look again and again. Back of the game, or beyond it, a dialogue is perused.

Emotional detachment, as interpreted by John Cage and Allan Kaprow, reflects the contention that artistic activity is natural to man, and consequently should not be differentiated from any other form of activity. One and all can be comprehended in terms of Happenings. Thus Kaprow writing on Spoerri lists, together with the artist's productions, the cooking of lasagna, lovemaking, sleeping, defecating. By stressing the chance character of Happenings at the expense of a meaningful sequence of events, the present is more easily detached from a historical order, and appreciated for its pure actuality. This in turn prompts a dissociation of conduct from any moral consideration. When before the 1964 Venice Biennale Rauschenberg was asked if he had considered at all refusing a prize, he remarked in mild surprise, "Who am I to say No?" A remark such as this makes explicit the difference in attitude from that of the orthodox Surrealist who is eager for an opportunity to defy the Establishment. Perhaps the most vivid illustration of difference between the two approaches is exemplified on the one hand by the Surrealist poet Jean-Pierre Duprey urinating in Paris over the tomb of the Unknown Soldier and, on the other, by Robert Whitman whose defecation is registered by a movie camera set within the toilet bowl for the benefit of the public in one of Alan Solomon's Happenings. Duprey's act is a desecration symbolic of revolt, while Robert Whitman's relies on the public's acceptance of "Why not?"

The "Why not?" attitude helps develop a sympathetic state of mind toward the gathering of information through the most unusual forms of investigation and experimentation. Insofar as art gathers and transmits information, the "Why not?" attitude toward art is healthy. Why not depict the dream? and introduce ready-mades and *objets trouvés* into an art exhibition? Why not imitate reproductions?

But art is not reducible to a means of conveying information. The statement has to be made with elegance. This is what Paul Valéry meant when he noted, "I stop saying in order to make." The object made by the poet or painter is one that the artist offers to the world. He is giving something useless as a compensation for not having worked at making something useful. The recipient will accept the gift if he finds it interesting and attractive. According to Sartre, the reader fills in the writer's statements with his own feelings, and Paul Eluard remarked, "Le poète est celui qui inspire." We do not just read a work of art; we read into it. Yet this is possible only when the artist has left something unsaid. He has to "stop saying" in order to withhold information.

By withholding, control is maintained. Without control there could be no civilization. Its prerequisite may be sphincter control, but the Sphinx is the symbol of its achievement. Gifts are compensations made for wealth or knowledge withheld. There is no reason, however, for us to accept all offered gifts. To extend permissiveness to the point where producing a sculp-

ture or defecation is not qualitatively differentiated
reduces the human being to the level of those dumb
animals for which all functions—copulating, eating,
sleeping, and defecating—are equal events or happenings.

In the world of happenings, love is nothing more
than an encounter and an acquiescence. Striking in
John Cage's book *Silence* is the total absence of any
reference to love, despite its wide range of topics. This
might be due to the influence of the monastic discipline of Zen upon the author. Since Cage's upbringing
is Christian, of significance is the very fact that he is
attracted by a doctrine which, in contradistinction to
Christianism, ignores love.

Pop artists and their intellectual guides take as
little interest in freedom as they do in love. But one
form of freedom they are concerned in maintaining and
expanding is a by-product of the freedom of the press.
In the first place, it is the press that feeds them with
slogans and images. Viewed as a source of information, journalism's function is to transmit news as accurately and as precisely as possible. We may suspect
that absolute precision in nontechnical language is not
feasible. For myself, I had not realized the extent of
the difficulty of giving precise technical information
concerning such things as the color of a material until
I read an article on universal color language, in which
we are told that thanks to the Munsell tables the
color of a "yellowish brown rug can be specified with
the greatest accuracy as $x = 0.395$, $y = 0.382$, and
$Y = 35.6\%$."[2] Since no writer would be likely to
describe the rug in a room in this manner, and no
painter would match the color of that rug with such
a degree of accuracy, one's belief is confirmed that
art may well be a source of misinformation. Any
semantic attempt to account for the work of men like

[2] Kenneth Kelly, "A Universal Color Language," in *Color
Engineering*, III, 2 M-A, 1965.

Cage, Rauschenberg, or Warhol in terms of communication of information is beyond the point. Accuracy is demanded as a consequence of competition, whether in play or work, or to establish truth in the realm of justice or to discover it in the field of science. To the extent that a work of art is original, it cannot be measured accurately, for it does not fit existent standards.

The artist cannot but misinform about shape and color of depicted objects, for insofar as he is a poet he is a being who associates what he sees with what he remembers. Through association of the present with his past the poet remains himself, and avoids becoming just a worker or a machine. Because of death, the poet can never reconcile himself to a world in which man becomes the sex organ of the machine (Marshall McLuhan). Fear of death caused man to seek means of postponing the inevitable. In the age of mechanical speed, the poet's function is to invent delaying techniques. Historically, delay was elaborated in relation to rituals performed around the altar, for the function of ceremony was to delay the end, symbolized by the sacrifice. In art, both repetition of rhythm and lack of clarity delay the end.

Yet Andy Warhol declares how desirable it would be to resemble the machine. But of course! for then there could be no misunderstandings. Nor can there be any misunderstanding about the literal meaning of Whitman's defecation film. It seems that some of the organizers of the Happening at which this movie was shown disapproved of it, but felt it was unacceptable to act as censors. Likewise certain critics refrained from adverse comment on the movie lest they be accused of narrow-mindedness. It recalls the mother who does not scold her child when he defecates in her lap because she learned from her psychiatrist that the infant's act must be seen in terms of a gift to her.

The child needs to learn not to make the gift. But

how should the critic respond to the artist who says Why not film defecation? Or write a poem to the process as does Felix Pollak?[3] Or mold excrements as does Sam Goodman? In the name of the attitude of "Why not?" the critic's role would be likened to writing copy for the artist's publicity agent. Has not the time come when the critic should earnestly ask himself not only how permissive must he be but how demanding? My answer: As demanding as was the Sphinx when Oedipus was questioned.

[3] See *Kulchur* 18, Summer, 1965.

III.
THE
IMAGE

THE IMAGE AND POETRY*

"What we see in a mirror is an image"—CALAS

"The law of excluded middle: either an image is in the mind or is not"—WITTGENSTEIN

When Paul Valéry remarked, "I did not want to say but wanted to make," he gave expression to a modern poet's predilection. Already for Valéry's great fore-runner Mallarmé, structure took precedence over statement. The Cubist poets, Apollinaire especially, grappled with the dilemma. Cubism, let it be recalled, marked a turning point in painting precisely because it subjected content to the exigencies of a tectonic synthesis of forms and colors. Finally, since I. A. Richards interpreted poetry in terms of pseudo-statements, critics have been stressing technical achievements while dismissing "poetic truth." In a now celebrated passage, Richards wrote: "There is a fundamental disparity and opposition between pseudo-statements as they occur in poetry and statements as they occur in science. A pseudo-statement is a form of words which is entirely justified by its effects in releasing or organizing our impulses and attitudes; a statement, on the other hand, is justified by its truth, its correspondence, in a highly technical sense, with the facts to which it points."[1] Richards cited "o rose thou art sick"

---

* Reprinted from *Kulchur*, Spring, 1965.
[1] *Science and Poetry*, 2nd edition, p. 61.

, an example of a statement that cannot fit into any logical relation that would be true. He thus proved to his own satisfaction the inadequacy of the attempts of modern logicians to treat poetic truth on the model of general coherence theories.

In the name of logical empiricism, Alfred Ayer observed that Richards was not justified in claiming that science deals with truth when actually it deals with significance, that is, with validations in terms of a coherent system.[2] It is unnecessary to adopt Ayer's extremism to accept that a statement such as "Parallels meet in infinity" does not have to be true to be valid. The veracity or falsity of a statement cannot be a criterion for distinguishing the poetic from the scientific. To establish a workable definition of the poetic statement we should go back to Plotinus' understanding of poetry as the sensuous embodiment of the rational; yet in contradistinction to the ancients' beliefs, neither the logical statement nor the poetic one needs to be true.

The most brilliant analysis of modern poetry in terms of significant systems of coherence is probably to be found in R. P. Blackmur's essays on Yeats and Eliot. Where the idealist would have contented himself with explaining how Yeats had been influenced by beliefs in magic and Eliot by Catholic theology, Blackmur scrutinizes their texts for impacts that events of a magic and religious order had upon those poets. He makes us aware that greatness lies in dedication to a sensuous interpretation of a coherent system of wisdom (magic or religious). Eliot emerges as a major poet not because he is theologically oriented but because he added a new dimension to the poetry of our day by interpreting experience in terms of myths and rituals of deep emotional value. Undoubtedly, it is Eliot himself who with his essays on Dante and Baudelaire paved the way to the interpretation of

[2] *Language, Truth, and Logic.*

greatness in relation to an emotionally valid coherent system of ethics. One cannot help but wonder what Eliot's poetry would have been like had he been a staunch puritan.

Eliot, as is well known, is deeply indebted to the great French Imagist poets, the Symbolists. After the Revolution of 1789, France became the cultural center of Europe, unique for having made the transition from deism to atheism without passing through the iconoclastic phase of Protestantism. And it was in the post-Catholic France of the nineteenth century that the most daring experiments were made in the use of images in art and poetry.

If, personally, I find Richards' definition of poetry unsatisfactory, it is because of its iconoclastic approach. When Richards points out that "o rose thou art sick" is a pseudo-statement, he is implying that the poet is not truthful; yet, what Richards conceives as a false image is only ambiguous. Obviously, the adjective "sick" was meant to convey that the fading rose was to be associated with a suffering human being. The significance of this statement is not *whether* it is true or false, but *how* the image affects our understanding by introducing a secondary association. To grasp the double meaning, the coherence of the utterance had to be momentarily weakened. In other words, to achieve the poetic effect of doubt, an element of delay, however brief, was introduced into the statement. Since delay was caused by resorting to an image, it behooves us, perhaps, to examine the treatment of images by artists working in another medium, that of painting. We might recall that in classical Greece the verb *graphein* applied to both writing and painting: thus a fresco would be signed "written by" the artist.

With the realization by scholars that there were more ways than one of representing volume in space, imitation of reality became an inadequate criterion of achievement. It is in terms of differences in style (and structure) rather than in degree of verisimilitude (or truth) that representation needs evaluation. The anthropologist Lévi-Strauss comprehended paintings as structures homologous to reality rather than copies of reality. Like scientific statements works of art are seen as units requiring validation in terms of a coherent whole based on laws such as frontality, the "vera perspettiva," the open form of the baroque, the cubist matching of parts.

Unlike painting, poetry does not structure images homologous to reality but introduces images into a primary structure, the linguistic one. As to the difference between the scientific and the poetic statement with which Richards was concerned, it is more correctly seen in terms of identification as opposed to ambiguity. False identifications such as that of clouds with smoke by the child or the primitive may be seen by us as poetic. So might a proposition such as "parallels meet in infinity," provided one is unaware of post-Euclidian logic. What else is logic but a linguistic structure that introduces order where there was none? In the languages of the Western world, the basic unit of this order is the sentence.

As an image, whether of smoke or roses or parallels, obscures the progression of a phrase, so can an object disrupt the order of an environment. This may happen when a coffee grinder is included among a drawing room's objets d'art. However, if instead of considering this coffee grinder as an extraneous element, we focus attention on its configuration, it acquires poetic value which leads us to confuse art with industry the way the poet confuses human beings with flowers when he exclaims "o rose thou art sick."

(We must distinguish mixing from interrupting. We mix images taken from two different classes while we interrupt either monotony or disorder; a room decorated with similar coffee grinders set in a row would look dull, while one cluttered with odd pieces of driftwood would appear messy. For the sake of varying the sensory data [impressions], objects must be set in a pattern. In the instance of the coffee grinders, we would interrupt the order of repetition; in that of the driftwood, we would limit the impression of disorder by grouping pieces in accordance with size, color, shape, or texture.)

In poetry, to appreciate a work which includes lines such as "o rose thou art sick" or "I am the rose of Sharon," the poem's pattern of ambiguity must be recognized. (When woven with images, the poem can be rewoven in the structure of a foreign language.) Thus to understand the poetic value of "I am the rose of Sharon" these words need to be comprehended in conjunction with the following clause, "as the lily among thorns, so is my love among the daughters." Superficially, the contradiction between the sentence's order and the images is solved dialectically; but on closer examination we perceive that unlike the statement which follows a syntactic order, images here are lined up. By adding one flower to another, we gradually come to see a garden. In Solomon's song we mentally advance into this garden step by step by means of images which halt momentarily our comprehension. Thanks to the delay provided by the suspension of logic, the poet makes us visualize a young woman as delicate as a rose, as white as a lily, so beautiful that in comparison other maidens are what thorns are to roses.

When images are symbolic, they may lend themselves to interpretation in a different field of reference. This is precisely what theologians elected to do in identifying Solomon's beloved with the Church. Nothing of the beauty of the song was lost. The love still corresponds to a reality, but the reference is no longer to a physical reality, but to a metaphysical one. In painting, this sort of transfer tends to be less convincing, for it is the painted image that is homologous to physical reality and not the pictorial structure. It is thus more difficult to forget the sensuous quality of a Raphael Madonna or a Botticelli Venus than it is to dismiss the physical attributes of the Rose of Sharon. Conversely, we are unlikely to forget the metaphysical severity of a Byzantine Virgin and that of a Gothic Pietà and be enabled to see them in terms of human love, beauty, and suffering. In lyrical poetry the impression that logic has been suspended is mitigated by the musical effects of rhythmic patterns. Yet, we should not deduce that music is indispensable to poetry; on the contrary, sound effects are as secondary to poetry as words are to music.

If, like Valéry, the poet is more interested in "making" than in "saying," then the poet's sincerity ceases to be a prerequisite to the production of a poem. Personally, I would go further and claim that the renunciation of sincerity is a prerequisite of achieving poetry. When, stimulated by joy or grief, the poet composes sonnets, he must dissociate the beloved person from the images she inspires in order to fit them into the structure of his poem. This is tantamount to saying that, while composing, the will to write about his Laura must be stronger than the desire to possess her or the sorrow at having lost her. The will to "make" must overcome the temptation to feel. But often it is not enough for the artist to avoid sincerity; he must be willing to deceive.

In painting this is clear. For the primitives images are never completely dissociated from the subject they represent. He who possesses the image has acquired magic control over the man or beast that is represented. Hence if the possession of the bull is a prerequisite to a successful hunt, depiction belongs to the activities pertaining to the hunting and trapping. According to Plato, hunting is the art of laying traps, that is, of deceiving a potential victim. Moreover, painting for Plato is an art that deceives by inducing us to confuse the copy with the original model. Yet, fundamentally, it seems to me, to make images is to want to be deceived. The inherently deceptive quality of images is most obvious in dreams, for during sleep we lack the ability to distinguish images from the objects they represent. How deeply rooted in our phylogenic past is this confusion between image and object is symbolically expressed in myths such as that of Narcissus falling in love with his own image and that of Pygmalion falling in love with a statue of his making.

The era of magic—a phase of man's cultural development during which object and image are confused—is historically followed by the era of identification. From then on, images are resorted to for conveying information about people and objects instead of being used to affect the latter. The information conveyed by pictographs was either structured serially —like numbers—for accounting purposes or syntactically for communicating messages. In addition to denoting the occupations of men and enumerating their possessions, the size of lots was designated in geometric terms. On the basis of such data man came to see himself as "an all in the now" (Parmenides). It was on this Euclidian basis that Kant conceived of the world as a mental synthesis. Lobatchevsky's discovery, however, that Euclidian geometry is not unique forced man eventually to realize that "for something to be true it must be thought in a certain way," the implication being that man cannot have absolute faith in his sensory-perceptive faculties. Kant's great egocentric view according to which what was unified by the synthetic activity of thought was *ipso facto* true proved to be untenable.

The romantic's loss of confidence in the being's identity undoubtedly has its origin in the interpretation of the nature of man in dualistic terms. In poetry, with Baudelaire, the beloved becomes a "flower of evil." Novel as Baudelaire's images are, their symbolism is as understandable as those of Solomon or Petrarca. Non-Euclidian poetry starts with Rimbaud. Rimbaud frees man from cause and effect, the sign from the signified: "Je est un autre. Si le cuivre s'éveille clairon, il n'y a rien de sa faute" (I is another. The brass is not to blame if it wakes up as a trumpet.)[3] By displacing images (inversions) Rimbaud modifies the configuration of objects. In his poem "The Vowels," in which he invents the colors of vowels, U denotes green. According to a most plausible recent interpretation U suggests undone hair framing a woman's head like an overturned U; U is green through the association of wavy hair with the sea, as well as with green pastures and, via pasturing herds, to lice and back to hair.[4] "U, cycles, vibrements divins des mers virides,/ Paix des pâtis semés d'animaux, paix des rides/ Que l'alchimie imprime aux grands fronts studieux." Through a process of associations (or additions) Rimbaud constructs a picture that is denser than reality.

In counterdistinction Mallarmé constructs a poem floating midair between reality and abstraction. Both Rimbaud and Mallarmé are masters of what must be left unsaid for the poem to be "made." Rimbaud in the above quotation left out the key referent, that is, the woman, while Mallarmé in the lines to follow omitted a key word, "inspiration." E. Noulet convincingly interprets "drunken wing" to mean inspiration, and "flights that have not fled" to mean unborn poems which "remain like icicles on a frozen lake":

Le vierge, le vivace et le bel aujourd'hui
Va-t-il nous déchirer avec un coup d'aile ivre

[3] Translation from Rimbaud by Louise Varèse.
[4] Anonymous, "A-t-On Lu Rimbaud?" *Bizarre*, No. 21–22, Paris, 1964.

Ce lac dur, oublié, que hante sous le givre
Le transparent glacier des vols qui n'ont pas fui!

Translation by Roger Fry:

This virgin, beautiful and lively day
Will it tear with the stroke of its drunken wing
The hard forgotten lake which haunts 'neath the frost
The transparent glacier of flights *unknown*.[5]

The loosening of the syntax is the device Apollinaire uses to concentrate attention on imagery. He is wont to catch the commerce of ideas and images on an international scale. Scenes pass before the reader's eyes with the swiftness of a landscape flying before the windows of a train. The poet stationed before his Paris window receives messages from far-off places of macaws and one-winged pihis, of Cypresses of the Antilles and a pretty girl in Turin:

From red to green all the yellow languishes
When the macaws sing in their native forests
Giblets of pihis
There is a poem to be made on the bird that has
but one wing
We shall send it as a *message téléphonique*
Giant traumatism
It makes your eyes run
Lo, there is a pretty girl among the young women
of Turin
The poor young man blew his nose into his white
necktie
You will lift the curtain
. . . .
From red to green all the yellow languishes
Paris Vancouver Hyéres Maintenon New York

[5] The italicized word *unknown* should be replaced by the appropriate rendition of the French, i.e., "that have not fled."

and the Antilles
The window is opening like an orange
The beautiful fruit of light.[6]

The magnificent experiments of Rimbaud, Mallarmé,
and Apollinaire (to mention only the poets here
quoted) were carried on by the Surrealists in the
twenties at the level of the unconscious; from the
language of dreams, they made poems intended, like
the dream, to conjoin communication with action.
"Les mots font l'amour," exclaims Breton. Yet, Breton
is at his best when he suspends the irrationality of the
stream of consciousness for the sake of poetic structure,
creating poems homologous to dreams and prophecies.
The underlying violence of the Surrealist attitude is
exemplified in Paul Eluard's poem to Violette Nozière
who poisoned her parents so that she might go to a
ball.

ELUARD: DARING AND HOPE

When the Pelican
The walls of the house are all alike
A childish voice is answering
Yes, as a grain of wheat and the seven league
boots
On one of the walls there are the family portraits
An ape in the distance
On the other wall the door that changing picture
Through which I enter I
the first
Then the chatter beneath the lamplight
of a strange ill
Producing madmen and geniuses
The child has lights
Some mysterious powders she brings back from
afar
that are tasted with closed eyes
Poor little angel her mother would say

[6] Translation from Apollinaire by Francis Steegmuller.

With that tone of mothers less beautiful than
their daughters
and jealous
Violette was dreaming of milk-baths
Of fine clothes of fresh bread
of fine clothes of pure blood
Some day there will be no fathers
in the gardens of youth
All the unknown ones
The men for whom you are always quite fresh
And the first one
The men for whom you escape from self
The men for whom you are nobody's daughter
Violette has dreamt of undoing
Has undone
The frightful snake coil of blood ties.[7]

Breton's poem to Violette Nozière announces, "All the curtains of the world are drawn before your eyes," and refers to Violette's crime in a line which omits mention of the essential fact of murder for the shock effect of the image: "We slide there where your high heel of sugar trod."

The imagistic experiments of the French poets had a decisive influence on Ezra Pound and T. S. Eliot, whose own contributions to the development of imagery were to be made mainly in a dramatic context. Their concern is with depicting events. This dictates that the suspension of logic be woven into the paragraph rather than into the sentence. A new veil of mystery covers Beauty since Pound said:

"Les hommes ont je ne sais quelle peur étrange"
said Monsieur Whoosis, de la beauté

La beauté, "Beauty is difficult, Yeats" said Aubrey
Beardsley
when Yeats asked why he drew horrors

[7] Translation from Eluard by F.C.

or at least not Burne-Jones
and Beardsley knew he was dying and had to
make his hit quickly

hence no more B-J in his product

So very difficult, Yeats, beauty so difficult.[8]

Eliot produces some of his most dramatic effects by
inverting the time sequence. In "Death by Water"
(Part IV of *The Waste Land*), we are told that Phlebas, two weeks dead, forgot his losses: "Phlebas the
Phoenician, a fortnight dead,/ forgot the cry of gulls
and the deep sea swell/ and the profit and loss." To
the implied silence of death is opposed the continuing
sounds of the sea: "A current under sea picked his
bones in whispers." The information that the current is
picking his bones precedes that of his drowning: "As
he rose and fell/ he passed the stages of his age and
youth/ entering a whirlpool/." Lastly, we are told in a
line which alludes to the turn of fortune's wheel that
Phlebas perished during a sea voyage: "Gentile or
Jew/ O you who turn the wheel and look to wind-
ward/ Consider Phlebas, who was once handsome and
tall as you." Eliot undoubtedly had Cavafy here as
model. Cavafy creates a dramatic effect through understatement. Thus in his poem "The Gods Abandon
Anthony," Cavafy omits the information that Anthony
is to commit suicide by substituting for it progressive
understatements: that Anthony is *leaving* Alexandria
(active understatement) and that he is *losing* Alexandria:

Like one for long prepared, like a courageous
man,
say good bye to her, to the Alexandria that you
are leaving

. . . .

listen as the final enchantment to the music,

8 Canto LXXX.

to the exquisite instruments of the mysterious
company,
and say good bye to her, to the Alexandria that
you are losing.[9]

Imagistic poems free from all syntactical organization have been attempted, specifically by the Dadaists.
But images freed from sentence structure fall to the
ground as helplessly as wingless birds. Herbert Read
was inexact in remarking "a poem that is pure imagery
would be a statue of crystal—something too cold and
transparent for our animal senses."[10] On the contrary,
it is an imageless poetry reduced to pure logical structure that is transparent. Ezra Pound diagnosed the
difficulty when he said: "Poetry ought to be written
as well as prose."

Poetry is ethically meaningful when it treats funda-
mentals of the being's relation to his world. "Who am
I? Who art Thou? Where am I? Where art Thou?"
Emotion aroused by such questioning is expressed in
terms of change and continuity. The significance of
change was pinpointed by Heraclitus, who remarked
that we cannot bathe twice in the same river; the
significance of continuity was formulated by Parmenides when, in his rebuttal to Heraclitus, he de-
clared that "the being is a whole in the Now." The
Heraclitean viewpoint finds its perfect expression in
music and dance, while that of Parmenides is in
architecture. In the strictly nonfigurative edifice, such
as the pyramid or the Greek temple, we recognize the
embodiment of man's longing to be in the Now forever.
A musical performance is a unique event (at least
before recording was invented). The exact repetition
of the execution is as improbable as bathing twice in

[9] Translation from Cavafy by Philip Sherrar.
[10] Quoted by C. Day Lewis in *Poetic Image*, London:
Jonathan Cape, 1955, p. 130.

the same flowing waters. Conversely, we can bathe again and again in the same river as we can enjoy a new rendition of the same musical structure. For all its solidity the monument is exposed to the danger of destruction: A monument endures, falls, and may be remade. The question proposes itself: Does our life get repeated or remade? We want repetition in our fear that we and those we love will cease to exist. Repetition, which is a form of re-creation, finds its most apt aesthetic expression in the ritual. By developing a pattern of repetitions the ritual offers reassurance that the movement of life itself can be repeated. Unlike the reassurance obtained through repetition of the ritual, successive repetitions within the ritual of rhythmic patterns of words, sounds, and gestures suggest that the end of what IS (life or ritual) is being delayed. Since, however, the ritualistic series of repetitions must themselves come to an end, the perfect ritual is one that creates the impression that it has no ending and must—albeit with interruption—last unto eternity. Such is, par excellence, the Byzantine liturgy.

When emphasis is shifted from duration to interruption, a plot is woven into the performance at the expense of the ritual and a new art is born: tragedy. Tragedy deals with interruptions in terms of clashes of will (expressed in words or actions). The dramatic treatment of the plot is what distinguishes tragedy from a much older form of art, the epic. Narrative art, whether in the form of the epic or the novel, weaves its basic plot primarily in relation to a succession of events, obstacles, and only secondarily, if at all, in relation to conflict of wills. While the play's action develops in a setting that is both a wordly version of the dream and a closed form of the world, the novel represents an abbreviated version of the flow of life or an extended version of the stream of consciousness.

Unlike both novel and tragedy, poetry, in the strictest sense of the term, is plotless—the way abstract painting is nonfigurative. It diverts attention from heroes and events to structured images. To avoid imitating reality, plotless poetry imitates poetry the way music imitates music. Perhaps the most intriguing aspect of modern music is in the elaboration of inner contradictions in terms of interruptions, either by varying lengths of sound or by zones of emptiness filled with noises arising unexpectedly during a given performance (John Cage). Could not analogous results be achieved in poetry by contrasting images to zones of stillness filled with scribblings?

Since, in principle, all imagistic structure is poetic, the poet's problem is to decide which of the possible imagistic vocabularies corresponds to the needs of his temperament, as well as to the intellectual climate of his time. Movingly, Rilke has written of the poet as one who, from childhood on, is always sensitive to the pangs of solitude *(Notebook of Malta Laura Brigge)*. The questions "Who am I? Where am I? Who art Thou? Where art Thou?" become for such a poet agonizing questions.

It is by introducing images that disrupt the existing aesthetic order that the poet makes himself heard as a poet. Rimbaud carried solitude to the point where he could express estrangement from himself ("Je est un autre") with the force of a mystic poet. An estrangement that seems in our time all the more dramatic since psychology has accustomed us to interpreting inner conflicts in terms of Greek tragedy.

Yet poetry which has as goal the metamorphosis of an infrareality into a superreality, cannot remain the sole form of lyrical expression as some Surrealists would wish. Intellectually, the poet is able to justify in his own eyes estrangement and isolation from the dominant trends of his culture in times when he can take his desires and dreams for the equivalent of those of masses isolated and deprived of the cultural advantages of their society. But the empathy Rimbaud had for the Paris Commune and the Surrealists for the October Revolution arises from situations that do not have their parallel in the Western world after 1945. With the bombing of Hiroshima there grew the feeling that mankind was from now on at the mercy of uncontrollable forces unleashed by science. Today, however, the growing conviction that atomic destruction can be avoided permits us to overcome the Existentialist despair of the fifties and acquire new confidence in the world around us. On the technological level, we face the antithesis between the fear of the hydrogen bomb and hope placed in automation.

Man has become accustomed to the idea that he is a child of the machine. He is no longer impelled, as was the Futurist, to glorify engine power and mechanical perfection. Pop artists merely indulge in the advantages of mass production. The forerunner of a new imagistic vocabulary was William Carlos Williams. As Harold Norse pointed out to me, Pop Art begins with Williams': "This is Just to Say: 'I have eaten/ the plums/ that were in/ the icebox/ and which/ you were probably/ saving/ for breakfast/ Forgive me/ they were delicious/ so sweet/ and so cold.' " The poetic quality of what seems at first to be nothing more than a flat statement comes from a new type of inversion: instead of the meaning being delayed by the imagery, it is the awareness of the poetic structure that is delayed. Only on rereading the poem do we realize that the effect is created by the interruption of the narration by the insertion of the exclamation "Forgive me." The lyricism of the poem is indisputable, as vivid as that in Maiakovski. Yet the doctor from Paterson whispers trivia while the Russian revolutionary hails hyperboles: "If I were/ as small/ as the great ocean/ I should rise upon the waves tiptoe/ and wheedle the moon with my tide./ But, being loved, where can I go/ being as big as I am?/ In such a small sky/ such a love cannot hide." (To myself the beloved are these lines dedicated by the author.)

Poets and painters have come to share a common admiration for the poetic potentialities of mass products the way the Surrealists of the thirties did for the *objet trouvé.* A painter may retain the layout of the word SARDINES from a label on the can, while the yellow of that label may stimulate a poet-friend's interest in the color orange—an ambiguity artfully noted and subtly played up by Frank O'Hara in a poem characteristically entitled "Why I Am Not a Painter."

The romantic poet, fearful of the chilling effect of reason upon feeling, invokes the irrational: at one time called Mania, at others, Fortuna, the Voice of God, Inspiration, the Unconscious. For the Children of the Machine, chance more often than not manifests itself in the form of accidents. Since music, of all the arts, benefited most from recent mechanical inventions, it is not surprising that the most eloquent advocate of aleatory methods of composition should be a musician. Yet the more the artist seeks to hide from truth, the more science perfects its methods of decoding mysteries. The day cannot be far off when the psychologist will use the computer to analyze dreams; with the computer the most impenetrable ancient writings will eventually be decoded. Already gamblers use computers to foretell results of roulette and baccarat. Since the "autobeatnik" computer writes excellent random verses, it has become quite presumptuous of the poet to compete with it. Can the poet still believe that he alone is the creator of a unique form of orderlessness? What can the poet make that the machine cannot?

Valéry's "I do not want to say but to make," should not be stretched to mean that what a poet achieves could be achieved by the machine. Is it compatible with the essence of the machine either to "want to say so as to make" or to "not want to say so as to make?" Valéry interprets his own words thus: "It was the intention of making which wanted what I said."

But between his antithesis between making and saying, there is an inevitable interruption of "saying" for
the sake of "making." The question becomes: What
is it that must remain unsaid for the poem to be made?

The poet who NOW asks himself "Who am I?" does
so in an age outliving its Oedipal traditions. Oedipus is
the key figure of a world in which man discovered
that he is "a whole in the now." It was to Oedipus that
the inhuman Sphinx posed the question "Who art
thou?" And Aeschylus taught us that Man had to
sever ties with a pre-Oedipal past, dominated by the
cult of the Mother Goddess, when the mystical union
between mother and son became a crime as fearful as
parricide. But since it was uncovered that the tragedy
of Oedipus is re-enacted in every single man we
question the taboo of incest. In a poem inspired by
the insanity of his mother, Ginsberg ponders having
sexual intercourse with her as a means of recapturing
her love. What he loses is the reader's sympathy for
his deprivation of love. Too much of what Ginsberg
says in "Kaddish" sounds like a confession which
makes the reader feel embarrassingly close to the poet.
Confession is a repudiation of solitude. What con-
cerns us in Oedipus is his crime, not his intention. To
create a poem the author must sacrifice "saying" to
"making," and replace confession by experiment.
Now the question is: In the speech of the alone to the
alone what is left unsaid?—Too little, always too little
if the reader is not to be remade in the image of the
other the way Adam is to be remade in the image of
his Maker.

After World War I, confidence in reason was badly
shaken, and after the long era of concentration camps
confidence in sensibility was lost. No longer neurot-
ically attached to another, the poet became psy-
chotically detached. Man's mental climate turned arc-
tic and existential. In America poetry became action.

Projected by the breath, scanned with the beat of syllables, it is aimed at the ear to explode in the mind. Projective poets should hurl their typewriters onto the junk heap to let dictaphones and records carry directly the sound of utterances to their destination without having to pass through the deathlike silence of the written word. By stressing the significance of the utterance at the expense of the sentence, projective verse succeeded in loosening the poet's lines and giving them a Pollock-like fluidity. This is a major breakthrough. Like Action Painting, projective verse is best understood in terms of process. But the champions of action in art tend to forget that in science process is correlated to pattern. Process is to pattern in science what saying is to making in poetry.

Unless poetry is to be once again enslaved by music, syllables will have to be treated as parts of words the way fingers are treated as parts of the hand. Robert Kelly has attempted to introduce the image into projective verse (*Trobar* 2) by reinterpreting the succession of images in terms of rhythm. For the new rhythm to be violent enough to project the poem like a bomb, images will have to explode with multiple meanings. The crescendo in Breton's remarkable love-poem "L'Union Libre" is vigorous because his images have ambiguous meanings. Images acquire multiple meanings through associations to memories, whether conscious or unconscious. Lyrical poetry is a history-conscious poetry, extending into time the soul's cry of pain (the soul identified with breath, *animus*, by the Latins). Unlike lyrical poetry, projective verse is the ejaculation of a poet who confuses action with communication. If poetry is to be reinvigorated by images, it will have to be dissociated from utterances. Images are breathless. Breath can only blur the image.

Contrary to the position of Charles Olson, the champion of projective verse, poetry ought not to become epic in the name of objectivity; the poet should re-

nounce recounting the passing of life. This in literature
only the narrative can do—and no one has better been
able to cut up time and reconstruct it cubistically than
Robbe-Grillet in his *Le Voyeur*. Poetry, unlike the
novel, does not deal with time in terms of events, and,
unlike painting, does not describe objects outside of
time. Consequently, the poet must focus his attention
on states of consciousness, more particularly on those
formed by series of accidents cut up and reconstructed
into new patterns and rhythms. The Surrealist concern
with the conscious resort to the unconscious and to the
"objective hazard" paved the way for contemporary
interest in objective situations. The younger poets' cool
attitude towards emotion is less new than they may
think: witness W. H. Auden's magnificent poem to the
memory of Louis MacNeice entitled "The Cave of
Making":
". . . the dead we miss are easier/to talk to: with
those no longer/tensed by problems one cannot feel
shy and, anyway,/when playing cards or drinking/or
pulling faces are out of the question, what else is
there/to do but talk to the voices/of conscience they
have become. From now on, as a visitor/who needn't
be met at the station,/your influence is welcome at
any hour in my ubity,/. . ."[11]
While Auden views the state of consciousness in
the context of an event—the recent death of a friend—
the younger Americans succeed best in describing a
state outside time. In "Anger" Robert Creeley fuses
the state of mind with the expression of emotion:
"He is angry. His/ face grows—as if/ a moon
rose/ of black light,/convulsively darkening,/as if
life were black./"
To this he subjoins: "It is black./It is an open/ hole
of horror,of/ nothing as if not/enough there is/
nothing.A pit—/ which he recognizes,/familiar,sees/

the use in,a hole/ for anger and/fills it/ with himself, . . ."[12]

With David Antin the state of consciousness is enhanced by the awareness of the state of an object. In the following text the poetic quality of the lines comes from the double meaning (human and material) of the term body:

". . . take a glass of water/drop it on the floor/it smashes/it is wood and glass and water/ the thirst is not appeased/ a glass of water falling/is a falling body of water/and obeys the laws of falling bodies/ according to which/all bodies fall/at a rate that increases uniformly/ regardless of their form or weight/ . . ."[13]

In his extraordinary poem "Hatred" Frank O'Hara expresses the state of consciousness in the setting of what might be called "indeterminate logic." Here it is not imagery that carries the burden of ambiguity but the logical structure as is made clear from the opening strophes:

I have a terrible age and I part
my name at the seams of the beast
in a country of robbers who prepare meals
for a velvet church green with stammerers
and with cuckoos, with comorants and cranes.

I've tucked the rushing earth under my legs
so I won't have to turn my back on Sundays
and the morasses of ritual archers milking,
and I eat in a prison of bread and mortar,
I eat the stuff with wooden provocations,

. . . . .
C, Vol. I, No. 8.

[12] *Plumed Serpent*, 11.
[13] Unpublished.

THE POINT OF THE MIND:
ANDRÉ BRETON*

Within little over a year, we mourned the loss of some of the most explosive geniuses of our time: Le Corbusier, the master builder who freed architecture from the crushing weight of the past; Edgar Varese, the sire of sirens; Giacometti, the sculptor magician who broke down the barriers between beauty and terror. André Breton died September 28, 1966; he was Heraclitean. In the twenties he had upset Cézanne's apple cart by shifting interest from aesthetics to a point in the mind's eye where the contradictions between life and death, the real and the imaginary, the high and the low, the right and the left, the speakable and the unspeakable, are one. Leader of a group of vanguard artists and poets, Breton had his gaze fixed on what might be called the magnetic pole of super-reality. In a time of countless betrayals he remained adamant.

A few months before the war, Breton went to see Trotsky in Mexico to prove that the revolutionary poet and the revolutionary statesman had no difference of opinion when it came to defending the cause of freedom. Leon Trotsky, the eloquent exponent of the doctrine of perpetual revolution, conceived liberation in terms of a Marxist solution of social contradictions.

* Reprinted from *Arts Magazine*, December 1966–January 1967.

100

While wholeheartedly adhering to this thesis, André Breton felt that the poet's specific role is to produce emotional states in which the union between opposites is experienced as true. The pact between the two leaders took the form of a manifesto in which Trotsky accepted the doctrine so dear to the Surrealists—that at heart poets are anarchists.

Art historians are apt to view Surrealism as a form of escape from reality, reducing it thereby to a variant of the doctrine of art for art's sake. Surrealists refuse to surrender to the abject conditions of reality. Breton has said that an urgent task of the revolutionary poet in wartime was to write love poems. His *Fata Morgana* is a hymn to love written in America during the last war. During the same period, another Surrealist refugee from Nazi-dominated Europe, Max Ernst, painted his most visionary erotic weddings. For the Surrealists, words and colors are but a means of exploring the identity of opposites, while chance encounters and games without rules are events loaded with poetic meaning.

Sartre has criticized Surrealism for its failure to achieve its goal and produce the synthesis between opposites. He was thinking in terms of an aesthetic solution which Breton expressly excluded by postulating that the contradiction is resolved at the vanishing point of the mind's eye. Harold Rosenberg notes that the wealthy collectors' delight in Surrealist works proves that Surrealism's antisocial motifs are innocuous. The collector's criterion is surely different from that of the poet. All is well with oil in wells, and an oil painting is subject to aesthetic appreciation. Art historians and critics measure the Surrealist contribution in terms of a retreat from Cubism or an advance toward Abstract Expressionism; they are involved with development of style. Breton despised this approach. He was categorically opposed to purely aesthetic exhibitions of Surrealist works such as the one organized in Paris at the Galerie Charpentier in 1964. He was against the Establishment with its temples of modern art.

Breton was not an art critic. Exhibitions and books of friends were for him jumping points for literary fireworks and proclamations. He had a passion for youth and would read into first expressions immense promises. However, Breton insisted that the young live up to his expectations. The list of painters and writers who are indebted to Breton is impressive, from Miró to Alechinsky, from Benjamin Peret to Joyce Mansour. Impressive too is the number of those expelled from the Surrealist group. They were never condemned for aesthetic reasons but for the betrayal of freedom under the banner of Stalin, Franco, or Moloch, or for a cynical disregard of the bonds of friendship.

Work tends to alienate man from himself, and duty to estrange him from love. Through love we gain insight into others. Breton's heroine *Nadja* is a reincarnation of Héloïse visited by insanity. In poetry Breton went beyond Mallarmé, who merely flirted with chance. Breton gambled with chance. Chance is to the poet of an atheist era what inspiration was for the poet graced by God, while automatic writing is the Surrealist's counterpart of religious and psychoanalytical confession.

Influenced by the presence of the Surrealists in New York during the war, younger American painters adapted automatic writing and chance to serve pure art. Breton is no more responsible for this turn of events in the destiny of Surrealism than Lenin is responsible for the nationalistic character of postrevolutionary Russia. What nationalism is to socialism art for art's sake is to humanism. When the world is subtracted from art, critics supplant poets, with the foremost critics tightly isolating the artistic phenomenon from the world. An apex was reached when Clement Greenberg proclaimed that the great superiority of the New York school over that of Paris is its banning of contradiction in pictorial composition. Furthermore, Greenberg's statement implies that modern art has become post-Expressionist: to abolish all manifestation of contradiction the artist must sever ties with his complex-loaded self.

But what meaning for the world has an art that ignores the world? Art that is not read as an expression has to be seen as a representation. We have long been made aware by the De Stijl artists of the figurative aspect of geometric forms and patterns; with the Abstract Expressionists we have learned to appreciate indeterminate patterns. While Mondrian reformulated the golden mean in terms that were to suit the intrinsic needs of an industrial era, Pollock and de Kooning provided vistas of uncertainty which enable us to transcend the industrial order.

There is no such thing as nonfigurative art! In a challenging essay Lawrence Alloway recently analyzed the work of Noland, Stella, and some others in terms of the single image. Undoubtedly through repetition with slight variations of an impersonal geometric form or pattern or of an impersonal pop image, the observer is awakened to the presence of the artist who produced these repetitions. It is through a system of repetitions that these artists assert their presence. This is tantamount to saying that the function of repetition is to stamp an image in the mind's eye. Psychologically, the role of the image is to assert the existence of the represented. But as soon as we reintroduce the concept of image, the value of a given image has to be assessed. When the image becomes the focus of attention the erudite critic loses his pre-eminence, for the value of images is determined from a point in the mind which the poet sees best.

THE NEXT REVOLUTION IN PAINTING

"Painting is the last art still in manuscript form." This apothegm is by Marcel Duchamp, a virtuoso of the dramatic gesture, who had once scandalously included a urinal in an exhibition of art. The idea that a machine-produced object, a *ready-made* in Duchamp's terms, is no less beautiful than a hand-wrought sculpture corresponds to a Futurist point of view. However, unlike the manufactured object, a work of art is able to express feeling. Through his interpretation of material, whether stone or pigment, the artist conveys feelings about images, forms, and ideas. Its power of communication makes art a language. This is what Duchamp had in mind when he compared painting to a manuscript. On the other hand, by treating a ready-made as a work of art Duchamp drew attention to the mechanical quality of language, that is, its capacity for repetition similar to that of the machine which goes on repeating its performance. In this context writing is an apparatus which preserves spoken words in manuscript form. The ancients, including Plato, were consistent when they attributed the invention of writing to the Egyptian god of the arts and sciences, Thot. Whether Egyptian or not in origin, it seems certain that the earliest writing was pictographic.

What are the implications of the assertion that painting is the last art that remains in manuscript form? While multiplying it in volume, print displaces the manuscript, recording reproduces and repeats at will the original musical performance. Will not original painting be superseded by faithful printed reproduction? Some years ago André Malraux created a sensation when he dramatized the fact that the aesthetic judgment of artist and critic is to a large extent conditioned by works seen only in reproduction. Thanks to photography, we now have what Malraux aptly calls a museum without walls.

In this influence of photography on art, we find an unexpected confirmation of the economic law according to which the production of consumer goods is conditioned by the production of tools and machinery required for their reproduction. Viewed as an instrument of reproduction, Gutenberg's discovery of the mobile type affected, as we know, the production of literary works, encouraging the development of forms, such as the novel, which came to express emotions and aspirations of rich and poor literates. Less emphasis has been placed upon the effects of reproduction on graphic arts. Let us glance back into history. The invention of bookbinding in the eighth century, which made it possible to replace awkward and vulnerable scrolls with compactly set pages, gave rise to a demand for book-form copies of old scripts, primarily of religious texts. Illuminated manuscripts when bound enjoyed far greater protection, and this fact was conducive to painstaking craftsmanship and the unexcelled beauty of the illuminated psalters and Bibles.

When bookbinding encouraged the art of illustration, the invention of the mobile type was to free painting from the need to illustrate history, sacred or profane. Painting in the Renaissance became concerned with the imitation of reality. Engraving, however, which attempted but failed to create a satisfactory illusion of reality, was generally viewed as "the poor man's painting."

If painting is to become reduced to the status of a manuscript upon being reproduced as satisfactorily as is the written language, the original will lose its significance. So far, the reproduction of paintings has had the opposite effect; ever since copper engraving made it possible to reproduce great masterpieces on paper, the diffusion of copies helped both to make known the original and to swell the number of those wanting to see it in the flesh. With the invention and perfection of photography, this tendency received further impetus, so that today, owing to the industrialization of tourism, millions are accorded the pleasure of rephotographing works of art first known to them in reproduction.

As long as the original could not be reproduced in all its sumptuousness and delicacy, its pale copies, by suggesting its greatness, merely helped to spread its fame. When looking upon an engraving after seeing an Andrea del Sarto, a Rubens, or a Poussin, or at a photograph of a van Eyck or a Clouet, we see darkly what in the original we see face to face. However excellent is an engraving by van der Borcht or a colored reproduction of a Monet, we know it is only a copy. But will this always be true? What will happen in the near future if the reproduction of color and texture matches the original?

The perfecting of photography releases the artist from the necessity of painting likenesses and eventually from the task of imitating nature. Art's emancipation from nature occurred when science ceased to treat geometry as an image of physical space. With Impressionism art enters its non-Euclidian era. Art imitates art. If the painter's objective is no longer the imitation of nature, he has little interest in techniques used by Vermeer in depicting a pearl or by Rubens in approximating flesh. Since he is not interested in learning the art of imitation, he has no reason to scrutinize an original masterpiece in the hope of uncovering the secret of a technique not revealed by the reproduction available to him.

According to Edgar Wind, adjustment to the crude requirements of color prints is responsible for development in art of a stylistically regressive taste. This art historian considers that if a Picasso and a van Gogh suffer so little in reproduction, it is an indication of their inferior quality.[1] It would appear that if we made the difficulty of reproduction an aesthetic criterion of painting, the great work would become a summit waiting to be conquered by the color print. To Wind's reminder that "there is no Raphael without hands," I would oppose the above-quoted phrase of Duchamp. Wind notes sarcastically that Malraux's famous "museum without walls" is nothing but "a museum on paper." Precisely! That is where the reproductions of all manuscripts should be: on paper!

The painting and the reproduction have this in common, that they are produced on a two-dimensional surface. Perhaps the most significant single step in our times was taken by artists who discovered the potentialities of a two-dimensional surface. As Thomas Hess forcefully said, "By breaking up the surface, by making each section of paint insist upon its place in the visible scheme, the artist exalts the two-dimensionality of his work." Attention becomes focused on the manner in which the pictorial elements are juxtaposed, the way the yellow and the green affect each other, on the value of a face in the broader pictorial field when it is made green or purple.

Penetrating lenses made possible the re-evaluation of the detail. Shaken was the hierarchical order of values according to which the foliage of shrubs and the crease in the sleeve of a coat were inferior in importance to a face. The displaced and exposed details blossomed in full independence. The artist's creativity

[1] *Art and Anarchy* by Edgar Wind (New York, Alfred A. Knopf, Inc., 1964).

no longer includes forever reinventing on the palette a recipe of paint; ready-made paints in tubes and cans free him from this painstaking job, while from college he went on to borrow ready-made images from illustrated media. Paintings, including images printed in silk screen, are further narrowing the distinction between originals and reproductions.

The multiple uses of reproduction in the service of painting today may attune artists to the revolutionary step of painting for reproduction. Painting will then cease to be at the mercy of collectors, while artists will be liberated from the temptation to repeat themselves simply to satisfy the law of supply and demand.

IV.
CRITICS:
THE
SUBJECTIVE
APPROACH

ANARCHY AND EDGAR WIND*

With dazzling erudition and consummate skill, as well as with wit, the eminent Oxford professor Edgar Wind undertakes in his latest book[1] to present the humanist's case against modern art. One by one the author of *Pagan Mysteries in the Renaissance* retraces the growth of what he considers to be the aesthetic fallacies of our age.

Dr. Wind claims that art has ceased to occupy a central position; carried by centrifugal forces, it has spread itself far and wide and, through diffusion, has lost its density. No longer is it possible to say, as Plato did, that great evil is brought about by a fullness of nature, for art's great enemy proved to be mediocrity. Wind reminds us that already in the last century Jacob Burkhardt had pronounced mediocrity as the truly diabolical force of the world. From our ability to enjoy and react intelligently to a comprehensive exhibition of Picasso held in London one day and to an equally comprehensive one of Poussin held in Paris the following day, Wind deduces that "art has lost its sting." No longer connected with the vital energies of man, art became reduced to being merely "interesting." Wind thus sees fulfilled Hegel's prophecy that a time would come when the center of gravity would shift from art to science.

Personally, I fail to understand why *Les Demoiselles*

* Reprinted from *The Village Voice*, May 7, 1964.
[1] *Art and Anarchy* (New York: Alfred A. Knopf, Inc., 1964).

d'Avignon of Picasso are less closely related to the vital forces of life than Botticelli's *Primavera*; why Giacometti's walking figures are further removed from these forces than an archaic *kouros*. A forest of Max Ernst is far closer to the vital forces of life, it would seem to me, than a Ruysdael landscape. Wind sarcastically remarks that the only mythological figure that inspired modern art was that of a man with the head of a beast. But if it is taken for granted that Venus is a fitting key figure in the work of a neo-platonizing painter, is it less appropriate for a contemporary artist to resort to the Minotaur as a key symbol in a Freudian interpretation of vital forces?

Comparing Manet's *Christ Carried by Angels* (of the Metropolitan Museum) to a Mantegna on the same subject, Wind finds that the modern artist's weakness lay in his having painted for an exhibition, not for a church. Following this order of argument, it could be claimed that a Byzantine icon of the Virgin and Child is superior to any of Raphael's because the stylized icon has a transcendental quality more conducive to prayer and ecstasy than a naturalistic painting.

For those who, with Baudelaire, admire the demonic in art, would not the finest paintings of van Gogh and Picasso bear evidence that the spirit of evil of which Plato stood in awe is still the expression of the fullness of nature?

To prove that modern art is reduced to being merely "interesting," Wind traces the progression of centrifugal forces which have carried art to the periphery of our intellectual life. Taking his cue from Gide (who, incidentally, was as incapable of understanding modern art as he was of understanding Poussin), Wind criticizes Matisse for having produced an art shorn of mind, reduced to pure craftsmanship. But worse was to come: Art now claims to be purely experimental. As Wind sees it, this only confirms his diagnosis that the center of today's life is occupied by science. Yet the beauty of an experimental painting relies on the relationship between symmetric and asymmetric elements of the pattern formed during the process of painting. And if I am not mistaken, it is with sets of symmetric and asymmetric numbers that the scientist deals today in both physics and biology.

A philosophizing artist could well disclaim Wind's assertion that science has displaced art by holding that aesthetics have invaded science. The contradiction between these two positions is easily overcome if we agree that experimenting is a form of activity pursued by a wide variety of scientists and artists. Yet, according to Wind, the modern artist lacks courage in that he avoids taking risks. This is hardly true: by experimenting the artist risks everything, since his failure—like that of the scientist—can eventually be a total one. Where a gifted humanist painter might not have succeeded in producing first-rate portraits or landscapes, the gifted experimenter either succeeds or fails. His whole existence as an artist is perpetually at stake: after the failure of his latest experiment, can he retain assurance that he remains a painter?

To their wide public, the fears and tremblings of the artists are unknown. But was the situation very different in the Middle Ages when religion was the fundamental concern? How many, outside monasteries, were deeply troubled by the deadliness of their sins? If today art did not occupy a central position, Wind would hardly have noted the shallowness of the masses congregating in temples of modern art to view St. Picasso or St. Kandinsky.

Professor Wind's indictment of modern art is rooted in the humanist's allegiance to historically determined ethical values. But of all the gods man invented to free himself from anxiety, none proved more demanding than History. The romantic poet's love of ruins, Baudelaire's indulgence in the alienation of the senses, the Symbolist's fascination with dissociation, Gide's preoccupation with the *acte gratuit*, seen by Wind as symptoms of artistic decay, are actually heroic attempts to free man from History. To the art historian's analysis of the symbolic meaning of the language of art, the champion of modern art opposes the structural analysis of the artist's statement; to the scholar's reference to history, he will oppose the modern anthropologist's cultural patterns; and to the humanist's ethical values, the Promethean freedom from responsibility.

TRUTH AND E. H. GOMBRICH*

In this collection of essays on the theory of art,[1] E. H. Gombrich re-examines the relation of art to truth in terms of contemporary theories of communication. Gombrich wishes to provide the critic with scientific criteria for analyzing the language of art. Since the theory that art is the expression of emotion found its justification in Kant's concept of intuition, truth in art has been equated with sincerity. Expressionist theories and techniques have so influenced our taste that certain critics and art historians have downgraded well-known pre-Romantic painters for being dishonest although it never occurred to the latter that sincerity was a prerequisite of art. Apt, therefore, is Gombrich's reminder that in his religious paintings Guido Reni "did not want to express piety, he wanted to use the expression of piety, as he understood it, for a picture of a saint, and so the criterion of honesty versus dishonesty really does not apply."

Viewing the problem in more general terms Gombrich questions whether we have the "right to equate artistic truth with truthful communication." He reproaches critics like Roger Fry, Croce, and Suzanne Langer for confusing expression with communication. The difference, according to Gombrich, lies in the fact that expressions of emotions such as blushing and

* Reprinted from *The Village Voice*, September 23, 1965.

[1] *Meditations on a Hobby Horse* (London: Phaidon Press, 1963).

laughter are unlearned, being symptoms which occur naturally, while information is conveyed through signs and codes which must be learned, as they are conventional. Gombrich believe that art lies somewhere between two extremes, between the traditional symbols and emblems of religious paintings and those symptoms of emotions we detect in an artist's brushstrokes.

On the strength of this dichotomy, it is unacceptable to Gombrich that any mark the artist makes on the canvas should be viewed as a statement. The term "statement" should be reserved for propositions that can be true or false; accordingly the painter's red patch is not a statement unless it is interpreted in terms of other alternative utterances, the way we interpret the red traffic light as a signal which means it is neither green nor yellow. Gombrich objects to the Expressionist theory mainly because of its inability to account for structure in painting. He complains that the popularity of this theory "led to the cult of the spontaneous that we find in Abstract Expressionism and, beyond, to the uniformly blue canvas that expresses the artist's 'blues.'"

Ingeniously Gombrich explains how structure can be accounted for in terms of signals operating upon the alternatives reforming the recipient's doubt. He compares the artist sending his message to the beholder by means of his work to the code agreed upon by Theseus and his father Aegisthus to notify the latter whether the expedition against the Minotaur had been successful or unsuccessful. If Theseus was returning victorious, his ship would hoist white sails; but if he perished, the black ones would remain. The message failed because, having lost Ariadne on Naxos, Theseus in his grief forgot to change the sails. But, as Gombrich remarks, theoretically the code could have been perfected to provide more detailed information. If Theseus "had foreseen the possibility of failure in success . . . he could have indicated that he was victorious but sad by retaining the white sail but modifying its message by a black pennant."

To avoid the danger that a moment might come when "the message is muffled because of the many signals we are supposed to attend to" and therefore "no longer know which of them is intended to modify what," Gombrich proposes that we distinguish between dominant scale and modification as we do in Western music. In his example of Theseus the sail becomes the classifier and the pennant the modifier. An artist, Gombrich explains, may wish to modify a whole class of paintings, the way "Turner modified the traditional academy picture in the direction of the sketch" or the way Kandinsky modified a sketch made by Klee.

The urge to change what has been done previously and make new combinations can become a game that an artist may find challenging. Yet Gombrich does not draw from this the conclusion that art is a game. On the contrary he believes that the painter with a true artistic temperament wants the message to fit his mood rather than to subordinate his mood to interesting combinations. But what happens, we may ask, if an artist starts painting to express his emotions and becomes involved during the process in new combinations of shapes and colors? Has he ceased being a genuine painter to become a good player? Had he stopped painting while he was still expressing his mood would he have remained a true artist? Picasso has claimed that when he runs out of blue he uses red. Should we compare his attitude to that of the chess player who, having lost his bishop, attacks with his knight? In terms of Picasso's private code, is red equivalent to blue or second best? Could not this dilemma be overcome by adding to the distinction between painting and playing a third activity, one consisting in making artifacts, be it shoes, tables, or pictures? Making an object is not to be confused with moving a chessman or throwing a ball! If painting involves making, we shall have to conclude that the structure of a picture can no more be reduced to a set of signals than can the structure of a shoe or a table. The structure of a work of art and the structure of information are not identical.

We now may consider the alternative of whether the artist is obliged to refrain from expressing his emotions in order to make a picture. This is what Paul Valéry meant when he said that the poet stops saying in order to make. Is it not Theseus' failure to communicate that makes the story of his return so poetic? If the making of a painting involves failure to communicate, lack of information will be aesthetically an asset.

Discussing Gombrich's distinction between expression and communication, Richard Wollheim in an article published in *Art and Literature* (No. 5) examines the case of the artist who himself feels that he failed to express his emotions in the painting that he had just finished. Following a long and subtle analysis, Wollheim comes to the conclusion that we ought to make a distinction between expression of activities such as laughing, crying, or painting, and the elements in a painting that are expressive. The latter he calls "physiognomic links." Accordingly, Gombrich erred when he claimed that since we attribute physiognomic traits to given shapes and colors, we perceive them in a painting the way we perceive a man laughing, crying, or painting with dash. The physiognomic links or traits as perceived in a picture are actually pictorial signs that we interpret as symbols of emotions. Gombrich's statement that the artist's red patch must have a meaning "within the physiognomic context of his private world" is acceptable when we understand by this that the patch is the sign of a language that has to be decoded.

Gombrich ignores Suzanne Langer's concept of articulation when he states that Expressionism cannot account for structure. What else is articulation but a form of structure? Articulation is to the comprehension of the sense of movement in Abstract Expressionist painting what "significant form" is to the understanding of the static stylization of Cubism, geometric abstraction, and the contraction of forms in primitive art. In front of a Jackson Pollock we surely draw attention to eloquent articulation rather than to significant form.

One may achieve expression of emotion through articulation. To understand, however, the difference in mood conveyed by an Abstract Expressionist painting and a Cubist or a De Stijl, we have to compare them in terms of differences in patterns, and contrast the rigidity and precision of the Cubist pattern to the indeterminacy and looseness of the Abstract Expressionist one. But I fail to see what insight can be obtained by classifying the shift from tight patterns to indeterminate ones in terms of the musician's distinction between dominant and modified scale.

Through the study of Abstract Expressionism's articulation we come to realize that the artist may avoid completing a form in order to go on saying (by expressing himself with gestures). In other words the indeterminate pattern seems to correspond to a state of mind in which pleasure is found in identification of the self with the formlessness of signs that signify expression of emotion. To be convinced that the message transmitted through the painting is true, the beholder must be able to recognize the representation as one corresponding to his own belief about the represented—regardless of whether the latter is real or mythological, universal or idiosyncratic. We should bear in mind that the artist is not an external observer reporting in the metalanguage of mathematical signs, but an observer transmitting information obtained through his private experience. The truth of experience is measured in terms of intensity of belief, not in degrees of probability as is the truth of scientific statements (see Colin Cherry, *On Human Communication*).

Truth is not, however, the primary concern of the artist but of the historian, the lawyer, and the journalist. It would seem to me that the language of art could not be accounted for in terms of historical or legal reportage since art's function is not to imitate reality but to serve as a substitute for reality. Gombrich vividly illustrates the substitution theory in his essay "Meditations on the Hobby Horse." He explains that the hobbyhorse does not have to be an exact replica of a horse since what is required of it is that it should offer a substitute for riding. Likewise it is unnecessary for the stuffed doll to imitate exactly a baby, it being sufficient to have the toy cuddly and soft.

Analogically, an image used for devotion does not have to portray a lifelike saint, nor is an abstract painting expressing emotion expected to convey the perturbations of the soul with the precision of a cardiograph. To be inspired by a masterpiece we do not need to have it fully explained. We may admire a Crucifixion of Giotto for a variety of reasons, religious, aesthetic, historical, psychological. The scholar's faultlessness becomes a fault.

To sum up: Minimum credibility justifies the emphasis modern art places on an originality that taxes our credulity—the way "not saying" adds the mystery of silence to the work, the way interruption through saying introduces the magic of happening among forms-that-don't-conform.

TRUTH AND ALBERT HOFSTADTER*

The Existentialist philosopher Martin Heidegger overcomes the contradiction between saying and making
in art by accounting for the work ontologically, that
is, viewing it in terms of a creation. For Heidegger
the masterpiece is a manifestation of truth which lay
hidden in the creator before it was projected into the
world. He identifies truth with revelation, pointing
out that *aletheia*, the Greek word for truth, means
revelation. According to Albert Hofstadter[1] there is
nothing unscientific about Heidegger's doctrine because both semantic statements of R. Carnap and
ontological statements of Heidegger are assertions.
Hofstadter defines assertion as "a special form that the
human being takes on, namely, the intending of an
entity in the way of aiming to uncover it as it is." It
is doubtful whether any logical positivist would be
convinced by this Kantian interpretation. He would
refute the claim with: "Since I know that the supposi-
tion that 'what I think is true' may be false, the assertion that something is true does not include the
assertion that I think it is." It follows—as has been
explained by E. M. Moore over sixty years ago—that

* Reprinted from *The Village Voice*, October 14, 1965.

[1] *Truth and Art* by Albert Hofstadter, New York: Columbia
University Press, 1965; "The Origin of the Work of Art" by
Martin Heidegger, translated in *Philosophies of Art and Beauty*,
ed. Albert Hof and Richard Kuhn, New York: Modern Library,
1964.

by "true" we mean something which includes no reference to thinking or to any other psychological fact. If in our day the scientist is to concede that assertion can be used in cases involving psychological commitments, it will be on the assumption that whenever truth presupposes belief, the language in which it is transmitted differs from that of the scientist.

The doctrine that a work of art is a creation implies that art's truth is a pragmatic one, a truth about things in creation. Upholding this view, Hofstadter states: "In artistic representation the primary factor is presentation. Hence the important thing about a given work, say the horse of the Elgin marbles, is not that it is an image of a real horse but that it is a presentation of a horse." He explains that when we say that "something" is the image of a horse "this 'of' does not say that the image points out to a horse beyond it. It says, rather, that what is of import in a horse outside has been brought into the work." For Hofstadter "the only thing relevant about horses that is relevant to the work's meaning is the image that has been incorporated in the work."

If Hofstadter's analysis is correct we must conclude that the only thing relevant about the photograph of a horse is that it is a presentation of an image of a horse and not a representation of a horse, and also that the only thing relevant about a pornographic photograph or drawing is that it is a presentation of an image and not a representation of an event. Since the function of the image, both the language and dreams, is to represent, and since the purpose of photography is to reproduce appearances, manifestly representation is the primary function of images. Common sense dictates that the image conveying information about reality cannot be true the way the represented is true.

An image's function to represent should not be confused with its symbolic role, so often attributed to it. Conversely, because of man's capacity to recognize the difference between an object and its representation, we have been able to replace the represented thing by a symbol. Through systematic transfers from symbolized to symbol, man has been able to substitute illusion for reality and communication (through symbols) for action. Thanks to this transfer (in Greek, *metaphora*), events taking place in reality may be metaphorically represented on the stage or in stone, in words or in color. As Aristotle had it, this systematic transfer serves to purify the soul. Whatever truth is contained in Heidegger's view, a work of art as a creation and a revelation is more precisely accounted for in terms of analysis and sublimation.

From dreams and myths (the two basic metaphorical languages of man) we have deduced that a system of metaphors is determined by the intensity of fear or desire that provoked the transfer. Hence the truth of a metaphorical language should be distinguished from both scientific and pragmatic truth; it is the poetic truth communicated in the language of emotions. The meaning of the poetic message can be unraveled only in context of a situation which had provoked the crisis of anxiety that has been overcome through a transfer. Great art is always the substitution of tragic fears or passionate desires, while the most illuminating interpretations of masterpieces are those exposing the underlying emotional and ideological factors of the crisis.

Heidegger's godless theology of creation may well be rejected while we remain impressed by his interpretation of works of art. Yet, from his deep insights into the beliefs of Greek master-builders, or the prophetic visions of Hölderlin or Nietzsche, the conclusion cannot be drawn, as he does, that great art should be interpreted in cosmological terms. Temples and cathedrals undoubtedly symbolically express man's effort to fill the void of ignorance with aspirations. In our age, however, art is the projection of individuals struggling for a place in a highly competitive society. To interpret this art in terms of Heidegger's theory of revelation would be akin to choosing captains for transatlantic ships because of their ability to cross the Sea of Obscurity in caravels. What distinguishes the jet-plane pilots from riders of Arabian thoroughbreds is not greater courage but greater factual information. It is knowledge based ultimately on data concerning the structure of atoms and galaxies.

Like other productions, a work of art is an event, but unlike the product of everyday work the work of art is an event that "makes history," both in the life of the artist who gave form to it and of the community that accepted it. This amounts to saying that poetic truth is grounded in history. Since Heidegger and Hofstadter accept that history is best understood in dialectical terms, should not art too be understood in terms of conflict? Only those who believe that humanity is moving toward a future, eternal or temporal, in which all social and individual conflicts would be overcome can be consistent in viewing art as revelation of truth. Those who, like myself, do not entertain such faith must regard the work of art primarily as an expression of anxiety and doubt. This is why it is hard to be impressed by Hofstadter's interpretation of the horse of the Elgin marbles as the fulfillment of intentions and a revelation of the Greek spirit. An edifying subject of a sermon but poetically uninspiring! Anxiety, emotion, and doubt form the dialectical triad of poetry. When looking at the marble head of the horse that adorned the pediment of the Parthenon, can one forget that this is a symbol of conflict and not only of triumph? It can be contrasted to the wooden horse which marked the victory of the Greeks over the Trojans; the horse of the temple of Athena can be contrasted to the Cretan bull of Zeus!

No truce, whether between gods or cities, ever

solved basic contradictions. On the eve of World War I Chirico represented in modern terms the clash between two driving forces: the equestrian statue and horse power. More recently the basic conflict of the soul that Plato had depicted in terms of a chariot driven by a pair of horses, one tame and the other wild, appears in the domain of abstract art as an antithesis between the reduction of the expression of emotions to traces of gestures (de Kooning) or the denotation of the being's position in the Now either in relation to space alone, or to another alone in space (Barnett Newman).

ANXIETY AND HAROLD ROSENBERG*

Harold Rosenberg, to his credit, shifted the emphasis from the narrow perspective of formal analysis to the dramatic one of existence, paving the way to a reappraisal of painters as poets rather than craftsmen. Rosenberg's criterion is post-Marxist. Following World War II he offered Action Painting as an alternative to the travails of fellow-traveling. Later he was to set his Action-Painting theory in the perspective of the "permanent revolution" read backward. He thus accounted for the changes within the modern art movement in terms of the "tradition of the new." When new talent moved away from Action Painting Rosenberg lived up to his theory, lumping together Action and non-Action Painting under the heading Anxious Objects.

Taking his cue from Picasso's remark that "what forces our interest is Cézanne's anxiety—that's Cézanne's lesson," Rosenberg explains how, from Pollock to Guston, Action Painting unpeeled the content of painting till it unraveled anxiety itself. The approach is oracular, the tone Nietzschean. Two years ago, in "The Premises of Action Painting," in *Encounter*, Rosenberg, soaring with an aquiline eye over the vast expanses of Action-wrought surfaces, proclaimed that the "content of Action Painting is the artist's drama of creation within the blind alley of an epoch that has identified its issues but allowed them to grow unmanageable."

* Reprinted from *The Village Voice*, January 7, 1965.

It seemed to me that after the resolution of the Cuban crisis, we were justified once again in feasting our eyes with images instead of punishing our guilt-ridden conscience with aesthetic and the doing away with of color, texture, drawing, and composition until "content becomes everything." With keen interest I see in *The Anxious Object*[1] that some of the premises of Action Painting have been revised, while, at first glance, the article itself is unrecognizable under its new title: "Action Painting: Crisis and Distortion." While in *Encounter* Harold Rosenberg had stated that "the crisis that brought Action Painting into being has in no wise abated. On the contrary, all indications are that it has deepened, in regard to society, the individual artist, art itself"; in his book he modifies this to: "the crisis that brought about Action Painting has in no wise abated, though the political surface of the crisis has grown a bit calmer with the lessening of the threat of nuclear war." As long as Rosenberg adhered to the "Chinese" gloomy forecast of our world's future he was justified in claiming that, ever since the appearance in the late forties of Action Painting, "what has changed in the past ten years is that consciousness of the crisis has been further dulled—the increasing difficulty of dealing with it has probably furthered the spirit of abandonment. With the historical situation driven underground, the will to act has weakened and the inability to do so became less disturbing."

Once the danger of nuclear war had receded Rosenberg could no longer reasonably claim that the historical situation created by the imminent danger of the holocaust was driven underground; he therefore corrects the above quoted passage to read that it is desperation that has been driven underground. "Desperation" in this context undoubtedly refers to the drama of creation which had been

[1] Horizon Press (New York, 1964).

identified with Action Painting. But in a new perspective that encompasses among the anxious objects the targets and flags of Jasper Johns we can no longer speak of desperation. Whether he likes it or not, Rosenberg must accept the fact that Johns has to be comprehended in a set of pictorial references which include paintings of cigarette boxes, sculptures of king-size hamburgers, silk screens of queen-size flowers. As I see it, in the new pictorial scene desperation and anxiety have been replaced by temptation and seduction; the mental climate calls for snake charmers, not prophets of doom.

The Anxious Object fascinates: the image of a restless soul emerges, and the mind of a writer animated by a leader's contempt for mediocrity. Justly so! In art mediocrity is worse than injustice. In an article that first appeared in *The New Yorker*, Rosenberg lashes out against the "first bourgeois manifesto in the history of art with its call for mental and social security in painting." More revolting than revolutionary, this manifesto accompanied an exhibition of post-Abstract Expressionism in order to promote artists who disengaged themselves from their work. This exhibition included artists as personal as Al Held and Ortmann together with colder stars. Rosenberg was prompted to sneer. "To compare Held's *The Big A* with Stella's *Pagosa Springs*, a cutout of an H done in white and bronze parallel lines, like a radiator cover, is to clarify the difference between creative painting and what the Introduction called 'a sense of discretion and removal.'"

It is for their disregard of mental security that Harold Rosenberg undoubtedly admires Barnett Newman, Jasper Johns, and Saul Steinberg. In "The Labyrinth of Saul Steinberg" this great satirist emerges as the Charlie Chaplin of the cartoon, and Rosenberg's essay on him is a masterpiece.

I suspect that formalistic critics seek refuge in art

history out of fear of anxiety and temptation. The doctors of modern art, if too young to write about the five hundred years of Picasso, are now tempted to analyze anything that ops and pops before their eyes. Rosenberg is more than justified in denouncing formal criticism for having consistently buried the emotional, moral, and metaphysical content of modern art under the blueprints of achievements in handling line and color. He ridicules those who admire *Les Demoiselles d'Avignon* for having advanced Gauguin's ideas of color or Cézanne's means of construction. How much more than just formal elements must be included for a proper evaluation of *Les Demoiselles* is evident to all who have read Gombrich's analysis of the famous painting. This art historian retraces steps to show that in *Les Demoiselles* Picasso's achievement stems from the fact that "his private needs were transmuted into art." This raises the question: Though Picasso may want us to retain merely the anxiety of Cézanne, how is it that a painter who introduced the sense of art history into modern art is so anxious to dismiss all that he learned from Cézanne?

Transmutation and metamorphosis is stuff of which Beauty is made, while anxiety is the modern counterpart of Truth. It is Harold Rosenberg's privilege to be more interested in truth than in beauty, but is it sufficient?

V.
CRITICS:
THE
OBJECTIVE
APPROACH

DESCRIPTION IS NOT ENOUGH*

Interpretation is out. According to William Seitz in "The Responsive Eye" catalogue, "A nonobjective painting and sculpture defined a work of art as an independent object as real as a chair or a table." Objects need to be described. In the Bronze Age stored goods were described in the temple's inventories by pictographs, the earliest form of minimal art. With the development of economic life, man-made objects were increasingly treated as commodities which the merchant was called upon to describe. Clement Greenberg's talent for descriptive criticism might well be an outcome of his service at Customs where it is essential to check the correctness of the invoice.

By banning interpretation the formalist critic means to free art from all that is superfluous in the description of merchandise. Thus, William Rubin wipes out any Surrealist coloring that could blur his view of Chirico. Why would he otherwise contend (*Art Forum*, September, 1966) that "poetry and iconography aside, the conclusions Tanguy and Dali drew from his [Chirico's] work were further from its intrinsic meaning than was the painting of Mondrian." Intrinsic means within. Why should those interested in the "intrinsic" quality of Chirico's work isolate the inner meaning from poetic and iconographic elements? And why should a critic liken Chirico to the mystic

* Reprinted from *Arts Magazine*, Summer, 1967.

Mondrian whose rectangles have the golden section for inner meaning?

In the same issue of *Art Forum*, Robert Rosenblum informs us that, stylistically, Surrealism had been perfected by Picasso in paintings that depict that biomorphic side of life. Apropos of Picasso's *Nude on a Black Couch* of 1932, he deftly spins a yarn that could reconcile the most repressed spinster to Surrealism. This work allegedly illustrates a descent below consciousness, for "night, love and procreation are suggested by the hair which also becomes a kind of seed that touches an ovarian breast." The only state "below consciousness" that the Surrealists accept is the unconscious. To the rationality of the biomorphic growth the Surrealists oppose the irrationality of dreams.

The closest that formalist criticism comes to the understanding of the emotional content of a work of art is through the description of its sensory aspect. It so happens to be the way that commodities are most vividly depicted by their promoters; ads extol the softness or hardness of a mattress, the sweetness or dryness of a wine.

The Wittgensteinian O. K. Bouwsma tries to convince us that emotions are characteristics of a work of art. If true this would make it unnecessary to consider the work as an expression of the artist's emotions. Bouwsma says in his *Philosophic Essays* that poems, music, pictures evoke emotions as sentences evoke images. The question, however, is, Can art evoke emotions without recalling images? Thus the critics who write about the violence of Franz Kline's paintings associate this artist's famous broad black lines with the image of an artist painting with violent gestures, regardless of whether Kline himself painted this way or not. In other words, music and abstract painting evoke emotions when their auditory or visual patterns impress upon our mind an image that we translate in terms of this or that emotion or cluster of emotions.

For a critic to say that a work of art is sad or gay is as misleading as it would be for an astronomer to claim that the sun sets or rises.

Only when we view the work of art in a production sequence can we comprehend it as an expression of the artist's personality and interpret it in terms of his emotions and inner voices. But when we view the work in terms of a consumption sequence, we feel obliged to describe it as if we were writing a lengthy invoice for a pedantic client or selling culture to students. Art being the expression of the intrinsic, the great work of art is a revelation sudden and indescribable because impenetrable.

UNSUPPORTABLE SUPPORT *

Painting is structure of images or structure of signs. The minimalists by reducing art to pure structure make it impossible for the artist to express emotions. When Michael Fried claims that Noland and Olitski are painters of feelings, he does not explain how a structure of concentric circles, a pyramid of V lines, or a monochrome field are to be viewed as expressing feelings. Since minimal art structures nothing, Barbara Rose interprets it as being mystical. Yet minimal art consists of structures spread over canvas. What is mystic, that is, secret, about that? At least Michael Fried is more convincing when he views the canvas as supporting the structure. He is enabled to praise Noland for locating "the central point of concentric or radiating elements at the exact center of the support" (*Art Forum*, November, 1965); Stella for building "the pictorial structure on the shape rather than the flatness of the support" (*ibid.*, November, 1966); Olitski for discovering that the vicinity of the edge of the canvas is a terrain of extraordinary freedom and possibility (*ibid.*, January, 1967).

From a constructivist standpoint, Abstract Expressionism erred when it indulged in producing a rough surface of paint. In order to make painting completely intangible, Maître Olitski would like to spray the air with colors. Elated at the mere thought of such an achievement, Michael Fried points out that objects

* Reprinted from *Arts Magazine*, April, 1967.

of this kind would avoid the issue of pictorial structure, for there would be nothing literal in these paintings but paint itself. This is open to question. Since music which is intangible can give to sounds a structure with a sensory appeal, could not an analogous effect be produced with colors? Although Michael Fried does not produce fireworks, he ought to realize that luminous colors shot into the air have structure.

So obsessed by the idea is Fried that structure in modern art means structure of the support that he fails to note that Cubism, a forerunner of reductive art, structures images and not the canvas. In his quest for historical support of his thesis Fried might have paid more attention to the Futurists, who often used the frame as support of the paint. Frank Stella is undoubtedly a direct descendant of the Futurists and, through them, of the baroque artists who with stucco or color distort the appearance of a dome or a window. Reappraising the achievement of Greek sculptors who filled the metopes with statues, could we not say that they were support-conscious?

Lévi-Strauss' major contribution to our understanding of the antithesis between figurative and nonfigurative art consists in his tracing the origin of abstract art to painting and tattooing of the human face. From this position one deduces that the face is simultaneously the prototype of the image and of the design's support. Historically the substitution of the easel for the wall or the page marks the liberation of the image from the support of the edifice and the book. Unlike the image that *covers* the support, the decoration *adorns* the support (shield or canoe, blanket or jar, illuminated manuscript or rococo ceiling). While, in contradistinction to Cubism that structures the image and Abstract Expressionism that structures signs of gestures, minimal art structures its support. But can a support be structured and still remain a support?

Paintings that structure canvas, sculptures that structure the environment mark the destruction of artistic autonomy. Style for style's sake is being substituted for the doctrine of art for art's sake. In my view post-Expressionists can either restructure the image—as in the case of Lichtenstein, Rosenquist, D'Arcangelo, and Fahlström—or with Barnett Newman renovate the vocabulary of symbolic signs. Artists dissatisfied with the results obtained by reshaping the canvas will undoubtedly look for plastic substitutes. Plastic more fully than glass lends itself to the fusion of colors and support, opening the way for the creation of objects that are even lighter than are paintings on canvas. The recent experiments in Uvex of Les Levine point in this direction. In his shaped objects color and structure are one.

THE ENTERPRISE OF CRITICISM*

Clement Greenberg plays the game of art for art's sake with rules of his own invention. He proceeds on the assumption that, with modern art, the art of the Western world entered with a vengeance a phase of self-criticism introduced by Kant into philosophy.[1] Greenberg misleads when he explains that Kant "used logic to establish the limits of logic," for Kant treated reason as a phenomenon that had to be isolated so that it could be apprehended from without. Instead of accounting for his derivation of self-criticism from Kant's objective critique of reason or judgment, Greenberg limits himself to the unenlightening statement that "self-criticism of Modernism grows out of but is not the same thing as the criticism of the Enlightenment."

Is Greenberg refraining from saying that self-criticism grew out of the dialectical philosophy of Hegel to avoid the impression that his theory was modeled on a vanguard political theory of self-criticism? But Greenberg must know that Lenin had called self-criticism the criticism made from within the Bolshevik Party of its erroneous procedures. Instead of explaining how "Modernism criticizes from the inside, through the procedures themselves of that which is being criticized," Greenberg informs us that "'Kantian' self-criticism" (with the qualification Kantian here in

* Reprinted from *Arts Magazine*, September–October, 1967.
[1] Clement Greenberg, "Modernist Painting" in *Art and Literature*, No. 4, Spring, 1965.

quotes) "was called on eventually to meet and interpret this demand in areas that lay far from philosophy." One area lies not too far from God, for he cites religion "as an activity . . . that has not been able to avail itself of 'Kantian' immanent criticism in order to justify itself."

As he proceeds it becomes clear that Greenberg uses the term "area" to dissociate action from speculation, the practice of religion from theology, the practice of art from aesthetics. Self-criticism is arbitrarily conceived as a means for distinguishing serious art from art limited to entertainment instead of serving, as it does in Marxism, to coordinate action and theory.

The arts apparently might have shared religion's ghastly fate, for "having been denied by the Enlightenment of all tasks they could take seriously, they looked as though they were going to be assimilated to entertainment pure and simple, and entertainment itself looked as though it were going to be assimilated, like religion, to therapy." Luckily, self-criticism derived from experience cured the arts from the therapy of entertainment, for we are told: "The arts could save themselves from this leveling down only by demonstrating that the kind of experience they provided was valuable in its own right. . . ."

As is known, it was Hegel, not Kant, who viewed art as being conscious of its own self, that is, of its spirit. For Hegel, spirit is consciousness on the level of self-consciousness. From a Hegelian point of view it might be said that art enters a period of self-criticism when it apprehends its spiritual fulfillment by becoming conscious, through experience, of its historical development. For those, like Greenberg, who do not believe that art can achieve independence by pointing beyond itself to the spirit, art's self-criticism would have to be justified on a non-Hegelian interpretation of experience. Greenberg thought he found a solution to the difficulty in Dewey's theory, which holds that pure experience is an aesthetic experience: "for it is experience freed from the forces that impede and confuse its development as experience; freed, that is, from factors that subordinate an experience as it is directly had to something beyond itself."[2] But the "kind of experience" Greenberg has in mind is linked to a self-certainty acquired separately by each individual art: "Each art had to determine, through operations peculiar to itself, the effects peculiar and exclusive to itself." Hence "the task of self-criticism became to eliminate from the effects of each art any and every effect that might conceivably be borrowed from or by the medium of any other art."

Unlike Hegel, for whom art purifies itself through spiritualization, Greenberg claims that self-consciousness (renamed self-criticism) purifies the standards of quality of each individual art. Through self-criticism "each art would be rendered 'pure' and in its 'purity' find the guarantee of its standards of quality as well as of its independence." Greenberg does not find it necessary to remind us that standards used for eliminating outside interference should not be confused with standards used to determine inherent qualities of objects, as are the standards of measures and weights. Greenberg's so-called standards of quality are actually only criteria for defining a new purist style. But how is the choice of criteria determined by self-criticism? On the strength of Greenberg's own arguments the self that makes the choice is that of an art limiting itself to a technique of purification. Why does the technique of purification of painting or sculpture have to possess a self any more than does the technique of purification of metals or liquids? It would not be inappropriate to ask oneself what technician considers it advantageous to his self to adopt the criterion of technical purity as standard for criticism?

[2] John Dewey, *Art as Experience* (New York: G. P. Putnam's Sons, 1959), Chapter 12.

Greenberg concludes his pseudo-Kantian theory of self-criticism by proclaiming that " 'Purity' meant self-definition, and the enterprise of self-criticism in the arts became one of self-definition with a vengeance." What he should have said is that the critic who apprehends art from the point of view of the enterprise of criticism finds the fulfillment of his self by repudiating the impurities of the arts. This enterprise of confusing art with criticism has been assumed by Mr. Greenberg with a vengeance.

In the name of his enterprise Greenberg has recently admonished those followers of his who inch and pinch art to a mini. They have failed to take into account the important factor of "aesthetic surprise." This, says Greenberg, in a recent pronouncement,[3] "comes from inspiration and sensibility as well as from being abreast of the artistic times." According to Greenberg's doctrine of aesthetic purity it is through "Kantian" self-criticism that the artist is kept abreast of the artistic times; aesthetic surprise could then only be generated by the artist abreast of his times who is inspired to mix purity with foreign elements. It is in the name of aesthetic surprise that the mixtures of Rauschenberg and Oldenburg are to be praised and the purifications of the minimalists rejected with a vengeance.

[3] Clement Greenberg, "Recentness of Sculpture" in *Art International*, XI, 4, April 20, 1967.

SURREALIST PERSPECTIVE*

Superreality

With Impressionism, Cubism, and Expressionism, art ceased to be a pictorial rendition of reality to become the expression of transreality in which the process of making the painting is an integral part of the work. Surrealism focused attention on the limitations of physical reality. When Magritte included the inscription "ceci n'est pas une pipe" in a canvas with the representation of a pipe, when Dali portrayed Gala looking at herself without benefit of a mirror, physical reality shrank. Surrealists are not so much intent on escaping from reality and fleeing into fantasy as they are in incorporating magic elements into reality. Tanguy's deserts with their megalithic amoebas, Ernst's carbonized forests, Arp's sculptured hybrids enriched our vision with unique images. While the Constables, Corots, and Courbets refined our taste, the Surrealists opened our eyes.

Alienation

The Surrealists view the poet, whether writer, painter, or sculptor, as a seer in a world of iconoclasts. A great seer, Rimbaud, said, "Je est un autre." But what is it that alienates me from myself?

The concept of alienation is traceable back to the Book of Genesis and Moses' belief that, through sin-

* Reprinted from *Artforum*, September, 1966.

ning, man estranged himself from his Maker. When evil ceased to be interpreted in metaphysical terms, alienation began to be explained in terms of economic and psychological maladjustment. For Karl Marx, the worker under capitalism is deprived of the product of his hands which "means not only that his work has been transformed into an alien object . . . but also that it has become a hostile force in relation to him."[1]

According to Freud, society, in compelling man to repress his instinctual drives, paved the way to neurosis. Surrealism espoused both the Marxist theory of alienation and the Freudian theory of neurosis.

Metamorphosis

Their socialist convictions notwithstanding, André Breton and his friends in the thirties rejected utterly the pseudo-Marxist doctrine of social realism. In our day it seems more relevant to differentiate between the concept of superreality and the psychoanalytical concept of sublimation. Superreality is achieved through metamorphosis, without regard to whether these are sublimating transformations. Ernst's women metamorphosed into birds are but hybrid creatures. (It should be recalled that the term derives from the Greek word *hybris*, which means insult or outrage.) Dali's metamorphosis of a rock into a beast, Magritte's flaming trumpets, Brauner's androgynous boatmen are materializations, not idealizations as are the interiors of Bonnard, Vuillard, and Matisse. Surrealist works are intended to disturb, not appease; the Surrealist goal is unrest, not peace. "We have sufficiently represented reality, it is time to transform it" would be the Surrealist counterpart of Marx's famous dictum; "We have sufficiently explained the world; it is time to transform it." It is through images that repressed

[1] Arnold Hauser, *Mannerism*, New York: Alfred A. Knopf, 1965, p. 18.

desires combat ideology. In the language of art, the projection of images becomes an expression of hope. Hope, manifestly, involves more than the satisfaction of immediate desires. We can say, with St. Augustine, that hope that is seen is not hope, but the reverse could become a cause of despair. When we see nothing, we are apt to fall victims to anxiety. After Hiroshima man entered a new age of anxiety; the transformation of the world preached by the Marxist had either miscarried, as in Russia, or never materialized, as in western Europe. Inevitably, the intellectual community of the West drew the conclusion that contrary to Marx's assertion the world had been insufficiently explained to be radically transformed. In the wake of this sentiment, Surrealism lost the power of attraction it had enjoyed between the wars.

It Is

In the fifties, the official organ of Abstract Expressionism, the movement which in plastic art historically succeeded Surrealism, called itself *It is*, a reference to Bishop Butler's famous aphorism "Everything is what it is and not another thing." From this purely empirical point of view, the distinction between reality and transreality or superreality is irrelevant. Be it a painting, a chair, or a car, it is an object that is and not another thing. The role of the artist is to depict what he sees, and that of the critic to describe what the artist has made. Modern aesthetics should be based on the philosophical principles formulated by Wittgenstein. The latter wrote: "We must do away with all explanation, and description alone must take its place." In a recent essay on Andy Warhol, David Antin pointed out that since Wittgenstein has described the proposition as an "image of reality," the image could be viewed as a proposition about reality. Speculating further along these lines, we shall presume that the image-proposition about reality is formulated in linguistic terms. Since linguistic philosophy aims at formulating statements free of ambiguity, it follows that the images-propositions about reality should be expressed with the utmost clarity.

Le Roman Nouveau

Doing away with ambiguity and imprecision is the objective of Robbe-Grillet, unquestionably the most skillful and original novelist to have emerged since the war. By rigidly avoiding interpretations, by banning all metaphors, by depicting only what he sees without any expression of his own or anyone's feelings, Robbe-Grillet is able to boast that he liberated the plot from the trappings of drama. His *Voyeur* and *Dans le Labyrinthe* are subtle games in which the author plays with images reduced to propositions about men and objects. Undoubtedly, Robbe-Grillet assumes that his phenomenological theory of the novel is an alternative to the outmoded Surrealist dialectics of poetry.

As he himself asserts, Robbe-Grillet is antihumanist: His premise is that solitude is the condition of man and that theories stressing communion based on the hypothesis of a social pact are but fanciful metaphysical constructions. Yet surely if man is able to transmit thoughts and feelings to others, his condition is not one of complete isolation. (Man knows that he exists because language provides him with the means to make statements.)

The first question we need to pose when discussing fundamental problems of communication is: What information are we seeking or giving? The Roman Nouveau is minimal art in that it places the writer in the role of an observer who is noncommittal. Since the artist is not in quest of formulas and basic patterns, the premises of the minimal in art call for closer scrutiny.

Perception and Memory

We receive direct information about our environment from two distinct types of images, the retinal-visual and cerebro-visual (see R. L. Gregory, *Eye and Brain*). The latter are formed by coordinating the new information transmitted by the retina to the brain with information previously received and already computed by the brain. Without cerebro-visual images, we would not know that persons seen at a distance were not smaller than those nearby, that two walls seen at an oblique angle were the two sides of a square building, nor that the rows of trees bordering a road do not meet at a point of the horizon. This amounts to stating that seeing involves associating retinal images with remembered ones. Those who in search for objectivity want to reduce literature to what they conceive as concrete reality dismiss the function of the brain. In art, description and nothing but description is unjustifiable because retinal images are automatically associated with cerebral images. Artists who accept the contrary premise are as much victims of an illusion as are those who believe that painting and poetry can be reduced to automatic writing. Thus Robbe-Grillet, by omitting any reference to the passing of time, may have thought that he was dissociating what he perceived from what he remembered, when actually he created a unique structure of series of duration comparable to the structured space of Analytical Cubism.

In contemporary art the complicated tectonics of Cubism have been replaced by variations in patterns of redundancy. Optical effects produced by variations in the size of dots, in the spacing of concentric circles or rows of chevrons, the intensities of colored stripes, those retinal images are to art what flirtation is to love. The alternative is audacious juxtaposition. Confronted with Larry Poons' canvases in which he gives to musical scores the scope and playful facet of Pollock's Expressionist writing, we realize that here is a seer comparable to Miró when the latter merged a Dutch interior with a Matisse. Likewise, when Bob Morris defines space with blocks in the shape of projected cubes, we respond to the blending of De Chirico's illusionistic space with Wittgenstein's philosophical meditations on the appearance of the cube. On making this observation, the critic may permit himself to add that Wittgenstein is to thoughtful young artists of the sixties what Nietzsche was to the metaphysical painters of the teens.

Certainly Poons and Morris, thoughtful artists that they are, are in fact impure. Not clarity but ambiguity rules art, and Surrealism is the triumph of ambiguity —from doubt to paradox. In contrast to clarity, Surrealism cultivates depth. Complete clarity can be obtained only by avoiding depth. For Wittgenstein the goal of philosophy is the peace which can be achieved through complete clarity.

Solitude

Peace of mind may be experienced in solitude, as hermits discovered centuries ago. On rocky promontories and lonely oases they pursued the dialogue of the "alone to the Alone" (Plotinus). But this soliloquy with God feeds on tension and is an expression of anxiety caused by the hermit's belief that his flesh separates him from God. For the atheist, however, peace of mind implies a withdrawal that is total, corporeal, and spiritual, since he could neither send nor receive metaphysical messages—and peace would be indistinguishable from boredom. The mortal sin of artists in quest of clarity is the lapse into boredom.

Why boredom and not excitement? Excitement can be enjoyed even in solitude provided we are willing to associate our body image with objects of our erotic

desires. The union is metaphorical: we transfer (metaphora) ourselves into an imaginary situation, one that
is not but that perhaps was or *could be.* What is lost
in clarity is gained in intensity. Clarity of propositions and of forms (the good gestalt) is obtained
through successive reductions, in contrast to the series
of additions obtained through metaphors. Reduction
is isolation through purification, while metamorphosis
is a hybridization through participation. Participation
is exciting, isolation boring. To the clarity of the
proposition we should oppose the intensity of the
metaphor, to the meticulous description of the novelist, the penetrating interpretations of the poet.

Assimilation

In our day in the Western world intellectuals and
artists enjoy unprecedented advantages: our society is
assimilating all forms of expression and experimentation, tolerating deviant behavior, and providing ex-
perimenters in both science and art with material
security as well as applause. In this affluent and open
society, can Surrealism, which is an expression of revolt, have any prospect of a genuine rebirth? Perhaps:
provided Surrealism can raise a barrier to total as-
similation by opposing the covert to the overt, the
secret to the manifest. While science must probe for
knowledge, art can cultivate secrets, *mysticon* in
Greek. By cherishing secrets, as children do, the poet
can avoid surrendering to society. Surrealism is a cult
of the enigmatic adapted to a culture that has out-
grown the rituals and sacraments of official religions,
heresies, and metaphysical sects.

VI.
ART
IN
THE
AGE
OF
RISK

ART IN THE AGE OF RISK *

Now that the artist can do no wrong, a daemon might ask, Does it mean that he no longer bears any responsibility? In answer I retrace the genealogy of art in terms of liberation from ritual and religion, truth and imitation, from sincerity to self-expression. I am led to oppose risk to experience, and define risk in terms of a conflict between success and impossibility.

1. Purity

By freeing the spectacle from ritual, the Greeks discovered tragedy. In tragedies events are reconstructed in terms of a conflict between will and destiny. Aeschylus and Sophocles expose in their plays the horror of a law which demands that crime be avenged by crime. Even earlier, the priests of the young Apollo substituted purification for revenge. In contradistinction to rites that purify by their magic effect, a tragedy purifies through an identification of the spectator with a performance of an imitation of reality. Interpreting anxiety in terms of Greek tragedy, Freud paved the way for society to free itself from the cruel need to punish crime by crime; reform will eventually be substituted for revenge.

Purification through sublimation should not be confused with purification through religious confession. A writer of a tragedy and the painter of a somber

* Reprinted from *Art International*, February, 1968.

landscape may be able to produce a masterpiece without succeeding in overcoming their aggressive impulses. The value of a work of art is revealed in its expressiveness, while the importance of confession lies in repentance. Art is language; confession is a deed. The artist is the saint's antitype, since he may sign a pact with the devil.

Aristotle with his catharsis theory saved art from religion. When, under the influence of Plotinian philosophy, art was reappraised in terms of the sublime, poetry and prayer converged. A way out from this dead end was discovered only when Freud reinterpreted the Birth of Tragedy by internalizing the crimes of Oedipus. While Aristotle provided a classical era with an Apollonian justification of tragedy, Freud provided a romantic era with a Faustian interpretation of seduction. For the classicists of the Renaissance laws of perspective served to master the technique of imitation. As Picasso explained, Cubism was invented by artists to paint as they pleased, not in order to paint Cubist pictures.[1] Only an artist who believes that art is the expression of self would say, as did Jackson Pollock, that he paints with the canvas on the floor to be "in the painting."[2]

When a painting becomes the expression of self, the artist views it as a manifestation of his freedom. According to Hegel, "In thinking I am free, because I am not in another, but remain simply and solely in myself."[3] Does this mean that the artist who has identified pictorial thinking with the act of painting is to be regarded as a prototype of the citizen of Kant's republic of philosophers? Kant says that this state must have "a constitution of the greatest human freedom according to laws, by which the liberty of every

[1] "Picasso," *Cahiers d'Art* 1930–1935.

[2] In *Possibilities*, 1948.

[3] Hegel, *Phenomenology*, chapter on Freedom and Self-Consciousness.

other . . . is, to say the least a necessary idea, which must be placed at the foundation not only of the constitution of a state, but of all its laws."[4]

As Kant teaches that free will must act according to moral laws, artistic freedom would have to conform to them. It is not easy to conceive how abstract art could be said to either follow or transgress them. But we could imagine an abstract artist following the example of the infamous Ilse Koch painting works on the skin of human victims. It might be asked if, instead of painting for our edification the artist painted for our entertainment, would this be ignoring moral imperatives? This should be the opinion of Clement Greenberg, for he views modern art as having saved art from the danger of entertainment.[5] The implication is that we should a priori prefer the edifying art of David to the entertainment provided by Fragonard!

Far more important is Sartre's attempt in *Being and Nothingness* to overcome the contradiction freedom/morality by treating responsibility as a consequence of freedom rather than of moral law. Influenced by Hegel, who defines consciousness as consciousness of the self, Sartre postulates that "consciousness is consciousness of belief."[6] Hence his claim that the believing conscience is "the incontestable author of an event or an object" and must perforce assume the responsibility for the events and objects of which it is the author. This doctrine presupposes that identity is a synthesis achieved through consciousness of belief, and not, as logic teaches, a tautology. For Hegel consciousness is conceived as a process of development, since he views self-consciousness as being achieved through spiritualization of the self. Sartre, however, replaces that pure state of being the theologians call spirit by an infallible state of

[4] Kant, *Pure Reason*, chapter on Transcendental Dialectic 1, i.
[5] "Modernist Painting," *Art and Literature*, No. 4, 1965.
[6] J.-P. Sartre, *Being and Nothingness*, Part 4, Chapter 1, iii.

consciousness that somehow or other produces knowledge!

Dissociated from the Existentialist's mythical consciousness of belief, freedom is best comprehended as absence of bondage.

2. Truth

In the history of freedom, art would need to be traced from its bondage to religion to the conquest of its autonomy and beyond, when it undertook to question the value of its freedom of expression. Viewed as an expression of thought, art became conscious of its autonomy only after scientific and moral thinking had been liberated from religious thinking.

The philosophical discussions on the nature of freedom arose from the controversy between the Stoics, who viewed freedom in terms of freedom of thought, and the Skeptics, who viewed it in terms of freedom of action. As Hegel pointed out, both these schools considered freedom as freedom from bondage. Since Marx demonstrated that bondage serves to perpetuate economic inequality, the abolition of inequality has been made prerequisite for the establishment of a society of free men. From this assumption it does not follow, as Marx believed, that Kant's perfect republic will be the result of a voluntary association of free men. Marx's assumption that common interest is sufficient to dictate association is gratuitous. He ignores the role that aggressive instincts play in our decision-making. In this respect, Nietzsche, who postulated that civilization has its origin in crime, showed more insight. From a Nietzschean and Freudian standpoint one could claim that if man ever succeeded in abolishing economic inequality, society would be formed by a tacit agreement between those who wished to be ruled and those who wished to dominate.

Historically, thought is in bondage whenever the individual is crushed by the burden of collective responsibility. Primitive and totalitarian societies view the individual potentially responsible through association for crimes committed by a member of his family or his clan or his fraternity or his race or his religion. Under the weight of total responsibility art has to focus on solidarity as expressed in theological or political myths. Inevitably, in this mental climate images and patterns tend to acquire symbolic meanings, while techniques tend to be ritualistically standardized.

Art was liberated from its bondage to religion and magic only after man was freed from the fear of being held guilty for the misdeeds of another. This dramatic development took place during the seventh century B.C. in Greek cities of southern Italy. The new system of justice was epigrammatically formulated in a rhetra inscribed on a tablet that proclaims "peace and security to the kinsmen of the accused."[7] By this decree the aristocratic fraternities of the Eleatic cities were deprived of their power to apply the law of the vendetta and to condemn an innocent member of a clan for crimes proscribed by an unwritten tradition. However, the individual was bound to regulate his conduct, as Socrates taught, on the basis of moral principles. When he transgresses these laws he may suffer, as much as did Oedipus, from a sense of guilt. Alleviation from a feeling of moral guilt was provided mankind by Christianism which reinterpreted guilt in terms of sin. Sin, which is a spiritualized sense of guilt, can be absolved through divine grace.

As long as art's function was to imitate reality, it served to reveal truth. This explains how the art of painting came to be regarded by Leonardo as a science of knowledge which he aptly called *saper vedere.*

[7] G. Glotz, *La Solidarité de la Famille dans le Droit Criminel en Grèce* (Paris, 1902), p. 244.

3. Sincerity

Fusing painting with knowledge, Leonardo made of art a science, and not until Kant was art able to free itself from this bondage. Kant freed aesthetics from science by making a distinction between the cognitive elements of an object's representation and those elements of its appearance which we apprehend with pleasure or pain. Simultaneously, however, he bound both to psychology. His assumption was that the cognitive ingredients of an object's appearance are obtained through intuition, while the apprehension of forms is achieved through imagination. Historically, the significance of Kant's theory was to have enabled poets and artists to distinguish between investigation of truth and expression of sincerity. As Gombrich has pointed out,[8] with the Romantics art shifted from the description of truth to the expression of sincerity. But Gombrich does not mention that romantic art and poetry failed to create a literary and pictorial language adapted to Expressionist needs. Yet Rimbaud had pointed out that this was the weakness of Baudelaire.

The doctrine of artistic sincerity was undermined by Nietzsche, who claimed that the individual suffered from an inner conflict between two moralities. Nietzsche's insight was corroborated by Freud's reinterpretation of inner conflicts in terms of the id and the superego. Under the dictate of internalized ideals the ego projects repressed desires upon symbolic objects. Manifestly this transfer is at the expense of "sincerity" —the two concepts are incompatible.

Freud's discovery prompted Surrealists to give priority to satisfaction of desires over expression of feelings. Pushing to the limit Gide's fascination with the gratuitous act, the Surrealists would willfully confuse poetry with action in the name of "sincerity."

[8] E. H. Gombrich, *Meditations on a Hobby Horse* (London, 1963), p. 23.

Sartre, in mid-century, undermined the Surrealist position by declaring that the purpose of painting is to paint: For him, to paint is a manifestation of the freedom of an individual who in full consciousness assumes the responsibility of his acts. Interestingly enough, Alexander Liberman, perhaps under the influence of Harold Rosenberg, speaks of his dedication to painting in terms of an "experience of freedom." After stating that "to paint, or be involved in painting, is to affirm one's existence which has no validity without freedom," he discloses that he gave up hard-edge painting because it "limited too obviously the experience of freedom."[9] Liberman says also that the artist, within the limits of his canvas or sculpture, "can sense the total limits of freedom." It would seem from this that one should have to determine the order of limitation in the experience of freedom in art.

If for the Existentialist to paint is the purpose of painting, then to give up painting would be to give a manifestation of freedom. Does the artist stop his painting activity out of fatigue? Is freedom that tiring? Certainly this was the opinion of Mussolini, who once justified his seizure of power on the grounds that the Italian people were tired of freedom. Pursuing this type of reasoning, a psychoanalyst wrote a book expounding his view that Hitler's rule was the consequence of the German people's desire to escape from freedom.[10] A more rigorous diagnosis would have shown, I believe, that the Germans who accepted Nazism were escaping from responsibility, not from freedom. Likewise, it is responsibility that the child seeks to avoid when he is quoted by *The New Yorker* in the now famous quip on liberal education, "Must I do today what I want to do?"

[9] In introduction of catalogue to exhibition at Bennington College, 1964.

[10] Erich Fromm, *Escape from Freedom* (New York: Rinehart & Co., 1941).

The relation between freedom and responsibility was penetratingly analyzed by Emmanuel Lévy in an essay in his too little known book *La Vision Socialiste du Droit*.[11] Lévy justified the immunity enjoyed by worker and surgeon alike when accidents occur in the ordinary performance of their duties on the ground that the "employer" who hired their service tacitly assumes the responsibility for any risk. In other words, as Lévy explains, the worker's freedom from responsibility rests in his employer's confidence, that of the doctor in his patient's confidence. Where accidents are numerous and unpredictable, as in certain industries, it is of the utmost importance to determine who bears the risk.

In our highly mechanized society, risk is not only linked to accidents but also to failure of experiments. Only in an age when the artist was freed from the responsibility of having to imitate physical reality could a painter say, as did Braque, "How could I have made a mistake since I did not know what I wanted?"[12] To me this statement implies that, like the scientist, the artist explores the unknown. Certainly the present-day critic would have difficulty in taking Braque's paradox literally. A careful examination of an Analytical Cubist painting shows that the artist at least knew what he was *not* going to do. Undoubtedly the Cubists enjoyed the freedom from the responsibility of complying with what was expected of a painter. It may be assumed that each was able to rely on the confidence that his peers had in him. This, of course, holds true of any group of experimentalists.

Can we deduce that through experimentation the artist can "experience freedom"? I think not. To ex-

---

[11] Emmanuel Lévy, *La Vision Socialiste du Droit* (Paris, 1926).

[12] Quoted in *Le Monde* (probably from memoirs of Paulhan), p. v of Nov. 15, 1967.

perience freedom one must be free of the sense of limitation imposed by another person's confidence, or by the limitation imposed on oneself in the hope of obtaining the confidence of another, art specialist or fellow artist. Total freedom from responsibility can only be found in surrender, either to God, as with Father Zossima, or to Justice, as with Raskolnikov.

If the purpose of painting was to paint, the freedom to paint would be synonymous with the act. Hence a series of paintings by an artist would be nothing more than a succession of events. Why should these Action Paintings be of interest to anyone not personally involved with the artist's behavior or problems? Historically, the theory of Action Painting is an Existentialist counterpart of the poetic *acte gratuit*. The Surrealist acts spontaneously, interrupting the succession of daily events; the Existentialist paints by a succession of actions, mostly gestures, to form an event.

5. Achievement

Athens freed performance from ritual, while Paris freed art from moral imperatives. To the imperative "Do not!" of an academician, the artist could defiantly reply, "Why not?"

Why not dismiss truth and examine facts? Poets and artists began to do so with the robust sense of positivists. *Why not* replace the illusion of volume with basic geometric properties? *Why not* call this operation good (or beautiful)? Inevitably painting became a critique of the language of painting, the way poetry with Rimbaud became a critique of the language of poetry; Cézanne a critic of Poussin, Picasso of Velásquez, Miró of a little Dutch master.

Why not dismiss sincerity for experiments with symbols and the language of emotions and repressions? The symbolism of van Gogh, the colors of Matisse and Kandinsky, the signs of Klee and Miró, the images of

Ernst and Dali, the pictorial writing of Gorky and Wols are forms that Expressionism adopted in reaction to Mannerism. In modern art the pendulum sways between analysis of impressions of objects and forms (Mannerism) and objectivized expressions of states of mind (Expressionism).

Subjectivity can no longer be viewed in terms of Kantian elaborations of the statement "I think therefore I am." Contrary to what Descartes believed, this is not a privileged statement distinguished from statements of fact; its truth is not a truth of logic. "I exist if I think" is the logically true statement, as A. J. Ayer explains.[13] As he points out, the certainty of one's existence is not the outcome of an intuition that guarantees the truth of the statement. The certainty that we may have of our existence is the consequence of the logical fact that if one is in any state whatever it follows that one exists. I exist if I think; I exist if I paint.

Psychologically, the fact that an artist can say about one of his works, "I am the one who has painted it," may be as reassuring as being able to say when we look at our image in the mirror, "I am this person." Furthermore, the elaboration of a series of arguments or the composition of a picture provides one with the satisfaction of knowing that "I have done this" and "I have achieved this." It should be added: "I would not have painted it if I were not a painter," and "I could not have achieved it if I were not a good painter." The realization of the achievement can provide aesthetic pleasure.

6. Substitution

Although the artist, like the scientist, may have occasion to enjoy the satisfaction of a discovery or solution of a problem, the painter applies his innova-

[13] A. J. Ayer, *The Problem of Knowledge*, 1, iii.

tion to canvases again and again—like a variation on a theme. In those variations the artist recognizes with pleasure the stamp of his personality. It is the equivalent of the physiognomic resemblance that a father is proud to recognize in his son. Resemblance does not necessarily imply imitation, it may suggest only conformation. Likewise, when a painting is either an idealized version or a caricature of the sitter it can be said to conform to aspects of the person. An underlying structure deriving from the sitter is the common denominator between "photographic" imitation, idealization, and caricature. Cubism, by stressing structure at the expense of imitation, paved the way for artists to substitute structure for imitation.

The field of art apart, there are areas where substitution is more important than imitation. For religious ritual, for instance, it may be more important for a ceremonial ax to be made of jade and bear sacramental inscriptions than to be sharp or light. As pointed out by Gombrich,[14] for the child the hobbyhorse is primarily a substitute for the horse. It seems to me that both the unusable ax and the abstract hobbyhorse serve as substitutes because they are homologous[15] to the real thing since they reproduce its structural elements.

Both the ceremonial ax and the hobbyhorse are evaluated as being "good" only when they can be used in a specific domain, that of religious ceremony or childish entertainment. The instrumental value of a tool cannot be confused with its aesthetic quality: We may admire a given set of chessmen for their beauty and yet prefer to play with another. Furthermore, we distinguish in chess between the utilitarian value of a set and the strategic value of an individual chessman. Thus, a player may risk losing his knight

[14] E. H. Gombrich, *op. cit.*, p. 3.
[15] Georges Charbonnier, *Entretiens avec Claude Lévi-Strauss* (Paris, 1960), p. 96.

in capturing a pawn for the sake of improving his strategic position. The risks taken in games played according to rules are very limited when compared to the risks a painter can take in an age when art has been turned into a wide-open field of experimentation.

Looking at a painting of a Braque or a Picasso, the critic could well ask himself what the artist would have lost if instead of a curve he had put a straight line, or instead of one line three. The answer will be found in Picasso's famous remark, "When I run out of blue I use red." It is as if Picasso were saying that art is the art of substituting substitutes as well as being a substitute for reality. Since Cubism the critic is faced with the need to discover the method by which the artist substitutes substitutes to determine whether he is playing or not according to his own rules. Today, fifty years after Cubism, we have reached a point where we might ask ourselves if art has not become an antigame, a game in which the artist plays with structures instead of playing according to structure. Reappraised in this light, Duchamp emerges as the artist who invented structures for the critics to play with while he himself played chess.

7. Entertainment

Certain critics, influenced directly or indirectly by Carnap's theories, are claiming that art should be reduced to structure: they deny that art expresses, since there is no way of knowing whether others actually have sensations or feelings that are in any way like our own. The structuralist artists of today limit themselves to producing interesting sensory-perceptual effects. The most radical concentrate on a complex scientific planning and upon mechanical forms of reproduction. Others modify simple structures with a neo-Impressionistic sense of color.

From an empirical point of view the belief that the

content of a personal experience cannot be communicated is unjustified. The accumulation of data on the contrary suggests that there is a strong likelihood that basic experiences are the same for the majority of men. Art and poetry are forms of communication that have been developed through the ages because of man's conviction that his personal feelings and impressions can be made known and shared by others.

Communication is a substitute for action. On the most obvious level the master could never order others to follow his instructions. On a higher plane the same is true of art. Par excellence tragedy transmits the experience of others in a way that enables us to identify with actions and experiences not our own. Art creates what we might call a cathartic climate. Art could never have acquired cathartic power if reduced to communicating information. When art structures information poetically, it delays the transmission in order to entertain.[16]

The artist is always exposed to the danger of failing to *make* a work of art. The artist may not achieve his goal; he may fail by his own standards. His peers may see him as a loser. Art is an open game, and the weight of failure hard to bear because it is the image of his own self that is threatened and eventually destroyed.

There is no royal way of discovering truth; there is only the empirical way of finding out facts. There is no golden mean for distinguishing good and evil. What is good for the master may be bad for the slave. Besides the quest for truth and the pursuit of the good, there is the relief from boredom or anxiety that we find in the world of entertainment. In it, chance is opposed to boredom, surprise to certainty, memory relieved from fear through substitution.

In the age of risk success is the criterion of the good. But for those who attribute a priority to the distinc-

---

[16] See my essay, *The Image and Poetry* in Section III of this volume.

tion between two moralities, lack of success cannot be equated with evil and responsibility for the slave's failure may be thrown upon the master.

To artists who assume all risks to court success one might oppose those who have of art an anti-art concept. To the game of winning and losing on the canvas by substitution they oppose the knowledge that winning is impossible, because ultimately that which is being attempted is impossible.

Why attempt the impossible? Because we no longer believe in myths. Rilke sensed the impossibility inherent in art when in the *Duino Elegies* he defined beauty as "nothing but the beginning of terror we are just able to bear."[17] Could this beginning have been born when worshippers saw their Apollo advancing in marble? when Mantegna revealed the truth of Christ's death? when David re-created Christ's sacrifice in Marat's death? when Mondrian made of Veronica's veil a *vera icona*? when Max Ernst pressed from the dead wood of boards the breath of living forests? when Duchamp shrank depth to the thickness of transparency? when Barnett Newman made black and blankness cry for light? when de Kooning evoked the Song of Songs in siren pink?

[17] *Duino Elegies I.*

VII.
ARTISTS

ROBERT RAUSCHENBERG*

RR, 1961

Some painters say that the sea is blue; others say that it is not blue; for others, blue is spelled out in red, and there are painters who replace blue by an enigma. Ten years ago Robert Rauschenberg glued, stretched, or crumpled like a hide, newspapers dyed black. Whenever the hide did not cover the whole canvas he painted the naked portion black as well. Ever since the palette gave up shielding him the artist was mercilessly exposed to the blankness of the canvas. For the painter who is a poet, and therefore familiar with darkness, purity is offensive: *We now see darkly.* For RR blackness is not so much a color as a condition in which paper, paint, ink, canvas are to be found. Careful not to confuse painting with action, RR assembles different blacks, placing a glossy one alongside a rough one, a thick one, or a torn one, and fits them over the surface of the canvas. *We now see in enigmas* and do not know whether we shall ever see *face to face.*

From the blacks that do not form a single black we turn to a painting composed of seven identical white canvases. Inescapably the question poses itself: Which one is the whitest white? It is like asking oneself when facing one's image reflected in seven mirrors: Which one is me? *Seven Whites* is a self-portrait,

* Reprinted from *Kulchur*, Autumn, 1964.

yet even a self-portrait is the image of another. The poet's function is to spread doubt and create illusions. The illusion of greater whiteness or blackness is essentially no different from the illusion of a third dimension. But is the less white still white? Is the glossy black still black when it is next to a dull black? The relationship betwen illusionists in tridimensionality and color illusionists is analogous to that between priests and magicians. The worshippers of the third dimension, among whom should be included lyrical Abstractionists, such as Soulages and Rothko, are idealists, while artists who exploit differences between colors, as do Hans Hoffman, Kline, and de Kooning, are explorers in quest of disturbing results. RR will not accept that creasing paper is not a matter of color and that the combination of a creased black next to a stretched black is not as palatable as bread and butter. RR sets his seven white surfaces next to each other to show that they are as different as three apples by Cézanne.

(Since when did RR become a poet who explored differences? I am unable to answer this, as all antewhite and ante-black paintings were turned into ashes by two successive fires.)

Color being no more than a quality of paint, paper, or cloth, these materials are not to be subtracted from the painting, and must be treated as part of the pictorial content. Matter, as the ancients conceived it, is under the sign of dualism; for to comprehend it it must be divided. In this sense a painting which consists in splitting a given whole into fragments is a materialist one. To proceed by splitting is to follow an empirical method. It is this schismatic quality that distinguishes modern art from the art which is an imitation of nature. This non-Euclidian revolution started when the Impressionists interpreted colors instead of copying them. Painting has now become a process which includes the artist's handwriting as

well as colored material. Painting is no longer a colony
of nature and does not have to fit either into the
Ptolemaic universe of the Laocoön or into the Coper-
nican universe of Lessing. Painting is its own universe
of discourse. Unlike imitative art, which sought to
create the illusion of reality (human, divine, or sa-
tanic), modern art develops a series of relations that
convince us of the illusory character of the appearance
of physical reality. The art that does not imitate nature
cannot have sublimation as its function; its role is to
increase our awareness of the existence of other
alternatives. Otherness is more important than beauty.
"Je est un autre" (I is another) said Rimbaud. Modern
art is schismatic, and all that it proposes is heresy. RR
is an unquiet artist and he extends paper's creases
and the white's or black's split personality to the very
earth we tread on when he makes of dirt the content
of a painting.

Dirt is loaded with hidden meanings. A painting, in
the last analysis, is nothing but a surface that has been
isolated from its surroundings for the benefit of our
perception, in much the way a surface of the earth
is isolated for the benefit of a landowner. As life
springs from the earth, so meanings explode from
paintings. RR created a new picture instead of de-
stroying it, when he retained the green shoot that
sprang out of *Dirt*'s soil into our field of vision. *Dirt*
with its shoot is a new work in the sense that the ruin
of the Parthenon is new because different from the
original building. Today the Parthenon is a window
open to the past, but a painting hanging on the wall
should be a window open to views that have been
walled out.

RR went on to a series of pictures which included
plants, and during their exhibition would water them
daily. To see a painting as a window requires insight,
an awareness of what lies beyond our walled self. The
identification of paintings with a wall is for house-

painters who are in no position to cultivate our minds. Paintings, like plants, must live; they are alive when we let them change us and allow ourselves to accept our changed view of them.

The color quality of ink, paint, tar, paper, or metal is to modern painting what the object quality of iron, lead, wood, or stone is to modern sculpture. While RR's paintings are based on the division of the field, his sculptures come into being by the establishment of a continuity between two separate fields. One of his early objects consists of a stone lying on the ground and a vertical wooden pole, the two united by a length of slack string; another consists of a stone hanging at the end of a taut string, just above a little wooden platform slightly raised above the level of the floor.

Division may seem painful through its association with loss resulting from separation. When by means of a heavy stone and stout rope looped over a metal nail, RR anchors a block of wood, or when he lets a stone hang freely at the end of a string in a narrow box on a wall, we are able, through the missing image of boat and clock, to pre-empt departures and the passing of nostalgic time. No strings are attached to the stones that tumble among nails when we rock the container of the *Musical Box*. It is a sculpture, in the sense of a violin—baroque, feminine, and conversational; or a stone gong—magic, somber, mountainous, and authoritative. RR's musical box rattles secrets crushed in old chests, in the world of junk, where magic has taken refuge in this age of ready-mades.

The materialist doctrine, according to which all that happens is in the last instance due to chance, was refuted by its opponents on the grounds that if in a game of chance the lucky number came out four hundred times in succession this could only be due to the will of God. These arguments now seem puerile because, through the study of chance, man learned,

in his heliocentric era, of the existence of laws of
probability. But RR lives in the era of relativity. When
he composes a sculpture consisting of a heavy rough
block of wood and of twenty-one smooth rounded
pebbles in a heap on the block, and affirms that the
position of the stones can be interchanged at will
without altering the aesthetics of the whole, he is asking us to re-examine the relation of chance and art.
He appears to be denying that aesthetic pleasure depends on a strict order (in contrast to those who see
the beauty of mathematical formulas when they fall
into a neat pattern), for he has made use of the notion
that uncertainty is part of our delight. The indeterminacy in art, the *je ne sais quoi* that was seen as an
attribute of human beauty, has been extended, through
Abstract Expressionism, to the pattern, intentedly un-
identifiable. The artist who is sensitive to the indeterminate is a poet and, hence, essentially different
from both the worker and the gambler who are one
in their faith in tangible results.

To return to the paintings: Having extorted new
meanings from black, RR attacked red. Red has an
emphasis which both black and white totally lack.
Red is the most dramatic of colors, bloodstained,
regal; orange is a detail of red. In *Traffic Yellow &
Green* stripes of red alternate with stripes of yellow
fabric dotted with luminous green. Red paint drips
across the lines, traffic-wise colors clash with an ac-
cident-prone art.

A detailed narrative is touched on in *Hymnal*. An
old-fashioned worn-out hanging, sparsely painted,
has been turned into an abstract painting through the
addition of a few squares of material. A glossy red,
reduced to a few square inches, fights for our attention with velvet, once lush, now faded, dusty, and
intricately curvilinear, as were the events which may
have taken place in the parlor, too red for its size;
for a family too red, for their guests too red. It is the

pin-up red of a Valentine heart. The murky middle-
class interior has been tuned to murder: pasted in a
square in the lower left corner are the traits and
fingerprints of a young man WANTED by the FBI.
The crime may have been the outcome of a love affair,
for in one of the patches the name of a boy and girl
have been scribbled upon a heart. Bleeding paint is
pointed to by an arrow. Above, a photograph records
the victim fallen to the ground. Framed in an opening
cut in the hanging there hangs a mutilated copy of
the Manhattan Telephone Directory, the hymnal of
those addicted to the mysteries and perils of sex.
Hymnal is a detective story, or rather those elements
of one which do not reveal what actually took place
in the room with the omitted telephone. How small
this room with walls the size of a nightmare must
have been when the telephone rang and there was
no answer.

RR's collages have been said to derive from Schwitters, probably the most aesthetic-minded of the Dadaists, who was interested in dramatizing forms, and
"shows very conventional attachment to the values of
art," according to Lawrence Alloway.[1] RR, who shows
no attachment to the conventional values of art, is able
to dramatize the relation between form and content,
thereby giving a Surrealist touch to his collages. But
while the Surrealist compositions are riddles posed for
the detectives of the soul, RR's are dramas for diviners.

Gloria, Gloria, Gloria . . . without Vivaldi! Gloria,
long-necked like Botticelli's Venus, Gloria Vanderbilt
thrice a bride with her third man and his happy eye-
glasses. We have come to attribute a tabloid quality
to fortune, good or bad, and a fabulous heiress is not
compared to a Sibylla, as might have been the case
in the Renaissance, but is given to occupy a square
in a sensation-packed nickel's worth of news. Why
does RR reproduce the clippings of the fortunate

[1] *Art International*, Vol. 2, No. 8, 1958.

newlyweds four times? They gloriously occupy the upper left corner of the painting, heading a new chapter in the game of life.

This theme of Fortune opens with the lucky draw of four, the Venus throw of the ancients. The Diviner pursues his game: to the four he draws the ace, represented by a champion jumper, just below the fourth clipping. In the center of the painting there is an opening, a square hole cut in the canvas, for a snare holds together the isolated players. To its left we have deuces in letters, bold as advertisements, standing perhaps for BI (sexuality) and CO (pulation). To its right we see but a solitary gloomy face card amid nonmatching oblongs. It is the clipping of a nurse turned kidnaper. But enough of this dangerous game!

When we have learned not to perceive the difference betwen Vermeer and Mondrian, all signs are turned into images. *Painting with the Red letter S* is actually a portrait of S reclining in a red dress. S, the clue to serpents and secrets, is all that remains of the forgotten name on a can which secreted red. The artist who buys his paints cut-rate runs the risk of getting a wrong red, one too thick for canvas or too white for blood. Trade names, whether of vitamins or paints, are the Dada words of Manhattan's Babel towers. RR takes his chances with canned goods while trying them out as in this painting. Canned colors stop or cross or run into one another like cars and pedestrians. There is no way of knowing when encounters will be fertile or fatal. Tanguy discovered himself on his way to Damascus when he jumped from a tram at his first sight of a Chirico. But mystery does not necessarily lie in overturned Palladian perspectives of metaphysical painters. RR finds it in sweating walls of the wreckers' houses, on billboards with ads as mutilated as Babylonian tablets, in the ever-broadening gap betwen the lost and its remains. The artist defaces the handwriting on the wall. No reminders of legal consequences have ever prevented street urchins from adding moustaches to Miss Rheingold. Paints that come in cans with meaningless names are colors defaced, colors toneless.

Tonality is for nature, its sunsets, its waters, and its Impressionists. Atonality is in the hiatuses, in streets and blocks, in our skin and blockings. Empirical, unpredictable, magic is in the encounter of a green stain with a dark-eyed child. Images and non-images, squares and neckties are swept into the windblown path of paint, often angular, always expressionist. RR's style in painting and pasting remains too personal to permit a pattern, whether classic or baroque, to emerge.

This is equally true of his "Combines," as he calls his constructed works. A follower of Mondrian had once attempted to interpret the Master's work in terms of square pillars, forgetting that in so doing he was regressing to the sixteenth century, when the statue's mass made a hole in space. An abstract sculpture will fit into its surroundings by interpreting volume in terms of planes. RR did something else again when he translated volume into illustrated planes. He did it with the four vertical sides of the Combine named *Odalisk*. The pillar upholding the box—which is made of the lightest material, a transparent washing—rests on a cushion, as would an odalisk. The collage includes a photograph of two maidens bathing in the sun, giving nude body to an orange rectangle, an electric-chair candidate kissing his wife goodbye, an "Easter envelope," and a harp. Above is the symbolic cock. Easter the feast of love.

Unlike Surrealist objects that, however weird, always form a whole, RR's Combines give the impression of growing up distorted. RR distorts patterns, tattoos reality, vivisects hallucinations.

What has happened to the three beds of Plato, the ideal, or God's bed; the real, or craftsman's bed; the illusory, or painter's bed? Rauschenberg gives the empiricist's answer: "A bed is a bed is a bed." His bed is like a real bed, accidentally isolated from a line of ready-made beds, and like the painter's bed, for it has been defaced by an artist. In a face a beautiful scar is more beautiful than a Greek nose, Paul Eluard once remarked. Now that we know that man is not in the image of God, to the inapplicable divine laws and golden means the artist opposes accidents wrought with significance. The "what happened to that bed?" permits me to enjoy my bed and to forget that in my soul I'm closer to Raskolnikov than to Plato.

As accident is the devil's true name, in the world of art and accidents we need not fear the ghosts of Freudian castles, and can again reappraise the symbol. RR treats the accident as a lost object in need of a new identity. "Une porte reste ouverte ou fermée." RR presents a variant: we may alternate in folding the past and the future he suggests in the Combine *Interview*, a triptych whose two shutters can be closed but one at a time.

In *Monogram* the goat and tire are locked in a monogram. We think of an animal jumping through a hoop, of a sacrifice reinterpreted in terms of motor accidents, of the crowning of garlands, of Argonauts of the world of painting in quest of exotic masks. But these are bad habits of the mind. This goat and the defaced cock of *Odalisk* are objects whose symbolic identity has been rejected; they are to be treated as sphinxes, not as photographs of the unconscious.

In *Canyon* the stuffed eagle with a box for springboard spreads its powerful wings over its victim: the feathers of our dreams suffocated in a pillow. Now that RR has made a combine named *The Pail of Ganymede*, one may ask will Ganymede be the eagle's next prey? In *Canyon*, an infant, his arm outstretched, summoning, is lost in the artist's personal mythology. Jupiter metamorphosed into an eagle could well be

Robert Rauschenberg: *Canyon*, 1959. Combine painting. 86½ ″ x 70″ x 23″. In the collection of Ileana Sonnabend. Photograph courtesy of Leo Castelli Gallery, New York.

the patron saint of kidnapers. (A nurse kidnaper was included in *Gloria.*) The key to the solution is in the white and black keyboard framed above the eagle. Black for weight, 360 lbs. of it stamped on a vast field of darkness (upper right side), white for purity. The Statue of Liberty raises its hand like a helpless child whose name is Christopher. Will Christopher grow up to be free in the land of the free? The answer does not have to be given in terms of Jupiter, the bearer of Gandymede; or Christopher, the bearer of Christ; or of the critic, the kidnaper of meanings.

In *Inlet* a white heron takes refuge among outlets of electricity. Oh, the folly of white upon white! Above the heron is a minute seascape with a road running along the periphery of idle coastal land and then, the sea. Another detail is a photo of an eighteenth-century hero—migration into the past—set next to a pair of real-life work pants.

The heron of *Inlet*, the eagle of *Canyon*, the rooster of *Odalisk*, the goat, are we to see these as private totems?

Since 1958 RR has been in full control of his means of expression; he knows how to beat the life out of an umbrella and how to replace a rainbow by a necktie. He was taught that colors are not adjectives but has not forgotten that images too are words. There is no need for Expressionism to be either figurative or abstract for it can also be atonal. RR is one of the very few younger artists of the New York school who have not succumbed to the temptation of reducing mannerism to an empty gesture or to the lynching of colors on canvas. Modern art is a series of absolute beginnings, and artists who were brought up in an iconoclastic world have now brought about the desegregation of images.

When RR asked himself "What is black? What is white?" he plunged headlong into the world of paint-

ing. He emerged from this experience strong enough
to include the world in his painting. Surfaces become
denser, events more crowded. Temperamentally RR is
at the opposite pole of those who reduce the world
to an archetypal image, a square filled with deodorized
or vaporized colors. RR's squares are earthy, but his
colors are not plowed into patterns; his prototype is
not a worker, farmer, or housepainter, but an actor,
prototype of the imitator.

Art for art's sake came into being at a time when
painters dropped the heroes of Church and State for
the imitators of villains, for actors treated as performers performing, so that their gestures could be
included with the analysis of light, form, or expression.
But in an atonal frame of reference there is no way of
dissolving the act of performing into a series of Impressionist, Cubist, or Expressionist gradations. "Performing" must instead be isolated and treated as a
unique whole to be contrasted to other isolated
wholes, such as the color "red" or the word "caution."
In *Trophy for Merce Cunningham* RR juxtaposes a
photograph of Cunningham performing on the stage
floor to a gap between planks of wood, one of which
bears the printed inscription "Caution, watch your
step." If paint can be contrasted to a piece of cloth
why not "performing" to danger? The accident that
brings to an unexpected ending the series of steps
the dancer has watched himself doing over and over
again is a kind of event that can also interrupt the
performance of a policeman's duty, as is indicated by
the photographed fall of a mounted policeman and
his horse. What the words of warning are to the
photograph of the policeman's accident the Social
Security card studded with polka dots is to the dancer.

The world of the stage, although a closed one, is
not immune to accidents. The aesthetic value of
Trophy for Merce Cunningham does not lie in the
obvious contradiction between performance and ac-

Robert Rauschenberg: *Trophy (for Merce Cunningham)*, 1959. Combine painting. 66″ x 41″. In the collection of Mrs. William T. Sisler. Photograph courtesy of Leo Castelli Gallery, New York.

cident but in the treatment of an event, the accident, as a unit in a series which includes items such as printed letters and painted colors. In atonality the musicality of colors has been replaced by interruptions of colors and events.

In *Wager* RR traced his body faintly on the right board while standing with his back against the canvas. This way he contrasts the artist to the world of painting with its accidents, as denoted by the clipping of the sinking ship (central section). Politicians and sports fall within the field of the gamble. We have the photo of the Capitol (lower left corner) and of a KKK member (center), plus a football goal (middle foreground). The artist's portrait is hardly visible even in the original. Perhaps it is a reference to the fact that the painter had once included in his show a drawing of de Kooning which he had erased, implying that not to imitate an older artist whom he admired was the goal that he had set himself. How well de Kooning understood the meaning of RR's gesture is attested by his selection of a very good drawing for the purpose of erasure, thereby making the sacrifice more painful for RR.

By faintly tracing the outline of his body RR indicates his stand against imitation exemplified by the self-portrait—viewed as a copy of the mirror's copy of reality. This is the meaning of *Wager*: the artist versus the accident. RR gambles with patterns. The clipping of the ball game's goal serves as scale for measuring the proportions of the other squares. Seen in relation to its own square, the goal is a miniature version of the larger square formed, in the upper left corner, of a wood frame and a necktie. What a parody of the artist's goal! And repeated again with the horizontal line attached to a small black square set between the legs of RR's tracing of himself as a naked young man.

A true looking glass included in a work of an artist

who does not believe in imitation offers the beholder an excellent opportunity to reflect upon the meaning of reflections. In *Allegory* a mirror has been turned into a pillar bearing the twisted member of an automobile's carcass. RR overcame the uncomfortable sense of volume produced by the protruding mass of crumpled metal by shading parts of the mirror with a dull paint so that only the concave aspect of the bulging form would be reflected. It is as if the mirrored shapes drew back the car's Expressionistic bumper.

This veiled rectangular mirror is pictorially balanced by the circular veil of light, a red parasol flattened like a sun dial against a wall with one section sliced out in Matisse-like fashion. The parasol's missing piece, stiffened with paint, clings like a giant moth upon the wall of a private life. There hang too a pair of blue jeans which have lost their tight grip on the flesh, khaki pants isolated through emptiness, and letters of forgotten words and colors of forgotten yellows. The savagery of demolition has been retained, but the savor of the conflict between work and play has not been entirely lost.

In his paintings of this period RR guides the eye with the movement of brushstrokes. He is able thereby to preserve the isolation of pictorial units in a field that becomes more and more crowded. What is worse than an artist bound to his subject, crucifixion, square, or collage, unless it be the critic who reduces art to the squaring of crucifixions or collages? The artist's mission is to adulterate, and save us from boredom. In *Gift for Apollo* the god's heavenly chariot is chained; art is no longer carried away on romantic flights, it is held by the concrete as the pail's content indicates. In *Pail for Ganymede* Jupiter's cupbearer is replaced by a robot water cooler. When we turn its handle, in lieu of a fountain of water rising, a useless tin can ascends awkwardly up the ratchet. In *Pilgrim*, a chair forms part of the Combine to provide rest for the worshipper

with his back to the picture. In *Winter Pool* a ladder,
leading to nowhere, forms the central panel. "What
do you know about water?" says the painter of the
pool to the painter of parlors. "What do you know
about red?" says the painter of parlors to the painter
of pools.

*Gift for Apollo, Pail for Ganymede, Pilgrim, Winter
Pool;* art must be useless.

Wager, Allegory, Charlene are cityscapes: "Where
are we?"—Our New Amsterdam like the old one sees
itself in squares. The carefully irrigated flats of the
Netherlands modeled Mondrian's ideal city the way
Jerusalem modeled the Heavenly City. But New
Amsterdam is Babylon. All is confusion in Babylon.
RR precipitates, multiplies confusion, his thorough-
fares littered with wreckage of cars, debris of patterns;
squares bewildered by lights and sordid fetishes;
squares black, square blocks, square rooms visited by
vice squads; all the griefs Mondrian so neatly avoided
are included in RR's polyglot squares. In the red
delirium of an interior, color goes round and round
like an umbrella. Charlene! Fortune turns. Charlene!
Degas, Goya, Vermeer, seen through cheap reproductions become as tasteless as adult education.

In *Trophy for Tiny and Marcel Duchamp* the right
panel with its aluminum reflector must be for Marcel,
the dandy, while the left, with T & Y is dedicated to
Tiny. The glass of water with the spoon, the elixir of
water, is an allusion to the Duchamp glass and *The
Bride Stripped Bare by the Bachelors.* The middle
letters of Tiny's name have stepped into the central
panel between the necktie and the trousers. Visually
this triptych is a sheer delight with its patches of
resplendent red, with its intense sky blues and clouds
of white, with its yellow-white clouds and orange-
white clouds; clouds in skies, in mirrors, rainbows in
ties, clouds in sunsets.

RR is the painter of undecorated reality.

Half a century has elapsed since Futurism turned velocity into the subject of painting, but from the vantage point of supersonic speed how childishly slow is the movement of the Futurist image! If man is not to overreach himself in his attempt to conquer the universe, he must balance discoveries in outer space by the rediscovery of that *now* wherein Parmenides isolated the individual man. In turn he now can be isolated from the before and after. Painting is admirably equipped to free man from all associations with cause and effect. With cold precision RR abstracts objects from the here and there to make room for indeterminacy, so that another may participate in the happenings. Absurdity then becomes manifest.

The Illustrations for Dante's Inferno

Every imitation is a translation. Robert Rauschenberg translates Dante into the free verse of modern poetry. The nightmares poets poured into Hell are not only a source of secret delight, but a temptation to prod deeper into unknowns. By Minos! in and around Manhattan we have labyrinths and giants, centaurs and demons!—"No!" retorts the Critic, "I see racing cars, hulls of tankers, athletes on pedestals, soldiers with gas masks." Were he living in the fifteenth century this conscientious objector would have been incapable of mistaking Ghent for Jerusalem, a knight of the order of the Golden Fleece for a centurion, a Venus for the Holy Virgin. Twelfth-century Florence, Ghent in the fifteenth, Paris in the nineteenth were "absolutely modern" in the Rimbaudian sense of the term. The present must be dislocated if we are to have new visions of the past.

Accustomed, as we have become today, to *see* painting, we must relearn to read illustrations the way the Greeks read Homer on their amphorae and the Christians their psalms in illuminated manuscripts:

by keeping chapter and verse in mind. The illustration will not be true to the spirit of the poem if, for example, it "quotes" Fortuna out of context and presents her as the canto's heroine when the poet barely mentions her in one line. Unlike the medieval "imagiers," illustrators, since the Renaissance, have succumbed to the temptation to magnify the importance of an incident at the expense of the whole in order to box it into the third dimension. Fortuna be praised! In our day painting can once more permit itself to look flat.

The photograph provides us with the most convincing images of man ever since man was remade in the image of a photograph. The modern artist is a worker who takes into account the labor-saving devices our mechanized world has placed at his disposal; he feeds canvas with colors canned and nourishes images with illustrations culled from newsprint. As the illustration of a poem is a transfer of words into images, RR transfuses the blood of printed images upon his page. Poetic apparitions fill their space evoking that otherness which poetry recalls.

If the page illustrating a canto is to be more than a "chessboard" for the display of episodes—as it was so often for the medieval artist and is for the cartoonists of today—the figures and their activities must fill the page viewed as a single whole. Since the concept of narration in terms of "before and after" and "then and now" is intolerable in our time, narration must be perforated by discontinuity and studded by interruptions. With RR interruptions *are* color and blanks—irregular spaces over which the blank of a collage is occasionally superimposed for the sake of counterpoint. Through the analysis of dreams we have learned that discontinuity can be convincing.

As the transfer of images is achieved gradually, the artist is able to control the degree of clarity or faintness that he wishes to give to figures, creating thereby new and delightful aesthetic variations. RR uses those

Robert Rauschenberg: *Canto II*, 1959–60. Combine drawing. 14½″ x 11″. The second of thirty-four illustrations for Dante's *Inferno*. In the collection of The Museum of Modern Art, New York, gift of an anonymous donor. Photograph courtesy of Leo Castelli Gallery, New York.

variations for Expressionistic purposes, occasionally plunging the unbelievers into the fog of their ignorance and, at other times, granting the clarity of an understanding. In one section of the page sinners and evil spirits are ordered to come forth and others to vanish. Transition from one state of mind or from one scene to another is felt through pastel colors moving with the transparency of a melody. It is a deceitful motif, as back of it bestial forms devour our appetites with the immensity of fear, and cataclysms topple skyscrapers into fathomless pits. A shower of black strokes beats, strikes life in and out of an image. The picture lives, the poem has been transferred, the vision pulsates with the rhythmic beat of the pencil, used as an instrument of percussion. Hearken to Hell and the seisms of the mind!

The discontinuity of our life finds its ultimate expression in the photographic antithesis between still and action, active and contemplative life. The springer feels himself running during the long minute that precedes the starter's pistol shot, but the artist can describe the race in a montage of images.

Dante and Everyman who visit Hell must have their passport photograph ready to show when required. We see him (Dante or Everyman) as a naked young man, a towel around his waist, waiting to be summoned. In various episodes of Hell the young man is photographed in the role of athlete. The common denominator between poets and athletes is that they have style. Obviously the other great hero is Vergil. See him at the bottom of Hell (Canto 2) raising his arms, seemingly shouting in fury, because Dante still hesitates to take the plunge despite the presence of his guardian angel, the migratory goose, despite Miss America's offer of a beatific vision. Dante does follow Vergil and his presence is registered next to the poet as the arrow indicates. In the last canto Dante vanishes at the bottom of Hell only to reappear in an antipodian position in a great circle of light. To the right, in minuscule characters, are depicted Vergil and Dante, Vergil carrying the poet in his arms out of the underworld. These are tiny pictorial elements as compared to the main scene of the bestial three-headed Satan devouring Judas and other arch-sinners. The greatness of Satan's power is indicated by the power lines installed in his realm to assure the maximum degree of communication when the hour of his supreme struggles comes.

RR, 1964

From a consideration of Robert Rauschenberg's poetics interpreted in terms of his imagery in the earlier essay, I shall now proceed to a broader view of his work. The revival of imagery in vanguard painting is the important artistic manifestation of the late fifties. Like the imagery that had been introduced shortly before into poetry, it is a vernacular one. This differentiates it from Surrealist imagery, primarily symbolic.

RR is probably more conscious than any other artist of our time of the structural difficulties involved in the use of images in the language of modern painting. For a postclassical organization of actuality, independent of history and perspective, we must turn to Cubism—and it is to the Cubist tradition that RR belongs. Yet he proceeds from it enriched with knowledge acquired from painters who had expelled the image from their canvases. It is the sharpness of RR's observations that first drew public attention to his work.

Both Cubism and abstract art are tectonic. For dramatic effects those poetically inclined have to turn either to Surrealism or to German Expressionism; in the former, tragic situations are re-created on the level of neurotic complexes, while in the latter drama is drowned in the mire of emotions. Re-viewing

Cubism in the light of RR's most recent work, we recognize in it a first attempt to "edit" images. Like a newspaper, Cubism opposed current events to history. By contrasting areas of words and fields of images, the printed page of a great newspaper creates a beautiful modern asymmetry. In the age of mass production, the artist is led to combine ready-made pictures with ready-made paints. Yet gone are the days of meticulous embroideries of matchbox covers and theatre tickets, for with his huge screen images RR has triumphed over collage. There is virtue in seeing big. Picasso's great gesture with *Guernica* opened Cubism to the vastness of tragedy. Picasso, however, is the genius of a generation which was under the spell of the multifaceted images that photography and the cinema introduced. RR belongs to a generation showered with pictures which both adorn and litter interiors and streets. To imitate art, art now imitates reproductions.

It became necessary to exchange the compactness of the Cubist syntax for the looseness of Expressionist utterances for the artist to convey the impact that the four-colored cries of advertisements and loud-speaking picture magazines have had upon him. And only a young American is in a position to appreciate the broad variety of spectacles offered to his eyes, for he alone in the Western world has enjoyed the privilege of being brought up in a culture freed from countless Old World taboos. Cubism is both too compact and too studied to reflect that immediacy inherent in the actuality of the newspaper and sensed in the freshness of Impressionism and the vigor of Expressionism. Immediacy is perhaps most strongly imparted through discontinuity. It is discontinuity that gives style to happenings. In his compositions, RR uses a plotless sequence of events in settings of indeterminate patterns. With all the excitement and variety of the daily's front page he infuses the areas of pictorial space opened up by Abstract Expressionism.

Aptly, John Cage writes of RR's somewhat earlier works: "There is no more subject in a combine than there is in a page from a newspaper. Each thing that is there is a subject. It is a situation involving multiplicity. (It is no reflection on the weather that such-and-such a government sent a note to another.)"[2] RR wittingly captures the effects of simultaneity experienced when listening to a presidential speech or to a countdown at Cape Kennedy while glancing at the art and advertising pages of *Life*. The giddiness of those moments only the sea is quick enough to catch; only the dancer is able to stylize these shifts in balance. Style: the common denominator between poets and swimmers, painters and orators. Here is the style of a painter who turns each brushstroke into an image, every image into an event, and activates spaces between them. Here is a poet who washes out an image for the halftones of a silk screen to evoke a Rubens or the negative of a Rubens (see *Trapeze*). And, alongside, there are signs of the disorientation of an era in which man carries his struggle against gravity into the emptiness of outer space. However, RR excludes all extraordinary images so that they do not "run away with the picture," as he expresses it. He succeeds in preserving his images from fading into the oblivion to which yesterday's newspaper is doomed by presenting them utterly out of context. The imagery, so public in subject matter, does not tempt one to account for it psychoanalytically. The lasting impression is that the disposition of the images is due to felicitous chance.

RR's new paintings involve matching silk-screened areas with empty spaces. By setting some of his photographic images at variant angles, sideways or upside-down, he counteracts side effects, such as photographic

[2] John Cage, *Silence* (1961).

depth which might distract from the unity of the pictorial plane. The completed work embraces a series of additions and subtractions: the reduction of voids, the washing down of figures, the increase or decrease of pictorial density through superimposition of images. Layers of images rhyme with layers of colors, while double-exposure effects create gradations in transparency. With the silk screen, photographs, freed from their paper background, acquire a translucent quality which RR exploits to the full, creating various degrees of opaqueness and transparency. RR is exploring a whole new pictorial world. In one instance, in *Quote*, by introducing a diagrammatic representation of a solid between two views of a descending parachutist, RR stresses the transparency of space already present in the parachutist's painted background. A master of the dialectics of image-space, RR never permits himself to indulge in easy neo-Impressionistic scales of transparency; if the possibility threatens, he brings it to a halt. In *Quote*, he covers with brushstrokes part of an image (that of Kennedy) and blocks a prospective metaphor.

Ever inquisitive and experimental, RR has recently resorted to lithography to make a box version of a portfolio: the box consists of transparent plastic sheets printed with the silk-screen images of the stone plates. The order of the sheets can be changed at will by the viewer, producing every time fascinating effects of multiple images against varying degrees of translucency.

Both the transparent and the negative images are in fact images of an image. To what extent do they modify the true or literal one? A strong element of doubt has been introduced into the painter's statement—disturbing and subject to contradictory interpretations. But this is how it should be in the realm of poetry.

Robert Rauschenberg: *Quote*, 1964. Oil on canvas. 96″ x 72″. In the collection of the artist. Photograph courtesy of Leo Castelli Gallery, New York.

JIM DINE, TOOLS, AND MYTH*

How does the hat in the painting differ from a real hat Magritte might ask. When real buttons are added to the painted vest do we advance deeper into the meaning of art? This is a question Jim Dine raises by those works of his in which painted images and real objects implement one another. Dine proves that when real buttons are added to a painted vest they become false buttons. He blesses them with paint the way a priest blesses bread and wine with prayer. Confronted with Dine's adulterations we bear in mind that for the Eskimo feathers grafted to a mask live on it as much as on a bird; that for the monk garments of silverplate befit the image of a saint better than do painted clothes. Only the purist, objecting to the misuse of feathers, silver, and buttons upholds that it is not lawful for the painter to trespass the brush.

There is art in imitations of reality and magic in substractions from reality. Coming as a reaction to magic, Greek art devoted itself to imitation. In contradistinction, abstract art banned imitation, fearful lest the artist be confused with the magician. But the iconoclasts forget that images can no more be confined to mirrors and shadows, than feathers to birds and leaves to trees. May the day never dawn when painters are deprived of the magic power to rob reality!

Magritte, in quest of identity, queries why his

* Reprinted from *Metro*, Spring, 1963.

painted tree is not a tree. But when we now ask of Jim Dine what makes the co-existence of a black window and an ax a work of art, we are raising a phenomenological question. Braque and Schwitters translated in their collages pictorial propositions which had been developed in Cubist paintings. Dine bids us visualize the juxtaposition of actual tools and a canvas as a new unit.

A crisis in art broke out with the postwar generation of painters creating indeterminate forms. It accrued with the addition of figurative elements to the informal pattern by a new wave of the New York school. Unlike the realism of the Surrealists, the new realism which swells abstract art is not a protest against a mannerism. The new wave is not Dadaist: each artist, according to his idiosyncrasy, includes in his work the discoveries of his elders and paints in terms of broad empty spaces, incomplete patterns, erasions, and maculations. By reintroducing into vanguard painting the notion that a picture must "say something" a new lease on life has been granted to Abstract Expressionism.

Jim Dine has focused his attention on clothes and tools, two elements of our extended personality. With his series of oversized clothes he made a psychological transition from the world of Happenings, in which he played a prominent role, to the world of painting. He must have realized that clothes are the actor's principal "tools." Thus, painters of reality who portrayed themselves in extravagant costumes saw that the actor was the archetype of the imitator. There is as much dandyism in Jim Dine's imageless self-portraits with tools as there is in Rembrandt's turbaned self-portraits. The artist clothes himself in dandyism as the martyr does in humility. Only prosaic-minded painters profane their calling by making of the palette and brush, the tools of their trade, the main attribute of their personality.

Jim Dine, the grandson of a hardware merchant, manipulates tools with a child's aggressive handling of toys. He spills color over his tools: vises are coated battle gray, axes streaked with surf green, knives stained cherry rouge, oil cans brightened by international orange. torches extinguished in a heavenly blue, shovels daubed an inexpensive black. The glorification of tools is appropriate in a city where "the lonely crowd" works five days a week in order to seek refuge from mechanization by regressing to a playful handling of tools. Despite himself Jim Dine tempts us to unhook tools from his paintings and use them. The urge to drive a hole into a painting's plank is as great as that to hammer an extra nail into an effigy or to embrace Pygmalion's statue.

The artist is not a carpenter, for all that he makes must remain useless; that is why if he is to avoid remaining useless he must become a creator. Since it is with tools, knife, chisel, brush, or scissors that the artist creates, he will, despite the Futurists, always feel closer to Saint Joseph, the carpenter, than to James Watson the inventor. The artist can only be concerned with the conformation aspect of creation. With his brand-new machine-made tools, or ones renewed by a coat of paint, Jim Dine creates classical forms in contrast to those who manipulate the machine's carcass. Even in a work such as *Five Feet of Colorful Tools*, for which Dine resorts to thirty tools— some of them quite "baroque"—the general effect is classical for he tends to reduce to a minimum the irregularity of space between tools. *Five Feet of Colorful Tools* is a canvas dominated by a frieze of polychrome tools set against their bright gun-sprayed shadows. To avoid monotony the frieze is subdivided into four unequal sections by saws and a brace which extend slightly below the other tools.

Hammer Study, a frieze of Doric starkness, utilizes elements of objects and images in a rhythmic vari-

Jim Dine: *Summer Tools,* 1962. Metal, wood, rope, and string combined with oil on canvas. 7′ x 9′. Photograph courtesy of Sidney Janis Gallery, New York.

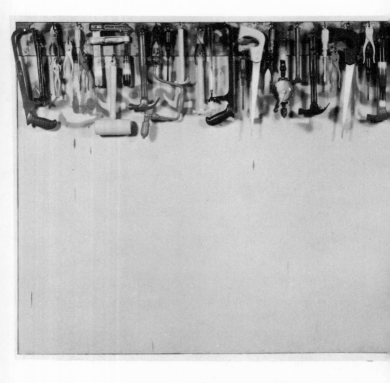

Jim Dine: *Five Feet of Colorful Tools*, 1962. Oil on canvas, surmounted by a board on which 32 tools hang
from hooks. 55⅝″ x 60¼″ x 4⅜″. Sidney and Harriet
Janis Collection Gift to The Museum of Modern Art, New
York.

ation on a theme. The theme is in two movements,
the first carried out by the progressive fading of full-
sized images, the second by a diminuendo in the running scale of eclipses. The last note of the first movement is simultaneously the beginning of the second.
The unity of the whole sequence is assured by its con-
tainment within the bounds set by the head and tail
of a true hammer.

In *Six Saws* the transition from object to image is
softened by the interplay between pairs of column-
like saws based on figure and ground. Jim Dine has
a gift for stylizing the displacement of real tools.

In *Colorful Hammering* a real hammer, streaked
with paint, hangs like a lifeless pendulum against
a Futurist ballet of its semblants, danced to the
tune of colors, shadows, and reflections. *Little Tools
Falling Out of the Canvas* expresses the swift flight of
a flock of tools pursued and given direction by a
painted arrow. Without the arrow rhythmic advance
would be lost, and the tools would be seen as pre-
cariously attached to the lower corner of an empty
canvas. In *Saw* the tripartite aesthetic unit consists
of a black canvas and the two parts of a saw, divided
by the picture's edge. The combination of a danger-
ously sharp instrument and a canvas heavily coated
in black dramatizes the conflict between production
and destruction, between painting and mutilation.

The portrait and the landscape are the bread and
wine of painting. Some of Dine's vertical pictures
constitute an understatement of the human figure.
Vise is sex caught in vice, while *Yellow Oil Can* is
vice-lessly suspended. *Red Knife*, stamped with the
word DEFIANCE, hangs as the symbol of a credo's fearful amulet. In *Window*, a window painted an impenetrable black is struck by an ax as was Oedipus
by the Sphinx's enigma. *T Plate* unbashfully recreates
a symbol of bodily suffering.

Tools in a Black Landscape, monumental and

leaden, comprises knowingly scattered tools: hammer, saw with pliers, scissors hemmed in by two pliers, a screwdriver, a wrench. From the workman's floor they have been elevated into features of a sculptured landscape. In *Crescent Wrench* a job has just been completed: the shiny bolts screwed into a board jutting out from a sky blue canvas recall a child's belief that stars are nailed to the firmament. *Sickle* hanging from a grinding wheel against a canvas of cloudy green is metamorphosed into a crescent moon, now waxing, now waning. Dine makes of the world of tools a microcosm which he explores with the meticulous care of a collector, entomologist, or gemologist. Pliers, with their elegant pincers, are assembled in a section of a vast flat cosmos in a composition devoted to *Some Chain-nose Pliers. C Clamp*, singly exhibited on a sheet of white paper, might have been designed to inspire a modern calligraphy.

Tools have served as the emblem of guilds and trade unions. Nails and hammer are part of the medieval coat-of-arms of Christ. In our time the hammer and sickle have been made into a powerful symbol. Jim Dine's understanding of tools is entirely personal. He is a sensitive and impassioned observer. His view, it would seem to me, is reconditioned by those hours of the night when sleep has been interrupted and the censoring of the unconscious has not yet asserted itself. He is a poet.

ALLAN D'ARCANGELO*

Before Allan D'Arcangelo there was Chirico to whom
we should be everlastingly grateful for having made
the landscape look as artificial as an African mask.
Reality is not enough! Playing with distance, Chirico
evoked a Palladian past. But he was not granted the
prescience to foresee that some half-century later his
biscuits would acquire a Pop taste. Is Pop Art actually
two-dimensional, as has sometimes been claimed?
With D'Arcangelo's highways Pop Art must seriously
consider the problem of tri-dimensionality. D'Arcangelo's use of distance neither serves to take us back
into a past of which Chirico was fond, nor to isolate
us in the present as does Dali. D'Arcangelo's highways
are as much in the *now* as Kafka's labyrinth. Unlike
the Futurist's view of speed which is spectator-
oriented, D'Arcangelo's is driver-oriented. One is
aware of having either to speed up or slow down.

The highway is today the significant form of the
American architectural landscape. Unlike Chirico,
who shifts the position of the vanishing point to create
the sense of loss of position between the now and the
historical past, D'Arcangelo makes of the vanishing
point the polar star of the speeding driver. When
caught in the straits of obsesssion, how is one to escape
from fixations? In his series of paintings called *US 1*,
D'Arcangelo approaches the dilemma by transcribing
perspective into the vocabulary of diagram: on either

* Reprinted from *Art and Artists*, October, 1967.

side of the highway, trees fall within a triangle; with
the parallels of the road, they meet the triangular skyline at a point we call vanishing .

Theoretically, these paintings should be too abstract to arouse emotion. But D'Arcangelo tunes his
paintings: the skyline is supported by jetting tree-
tops, the road is taunted by road signs which strain
toward the hyphenated center line; nevertheless, the
distant sky is precipitated into the foreground because
of the exaggerated clarity of the farthest road mark-
ings and trees. By omitting details which would distract attention from forms, D'Arcangelo takes sides in
the struggle between the abstract and its opponents:
road signs bear down starkly; daytime trees flatten
into chrome-green areas, after dusk night-green, while
black roads turn brown from the reflection of greens,
turned black. These defy the mirror of color.

D'Arcangelo breaks the hold of perspective by a
strict adherence to the driver's code. In a recent series
of works called *Barriers,* he weights his pictures with
constructions, whether beams of bridges coated in
primer-orange or warning signs striped white and
black or white and red, superimposing an irregular H
or a zebraic net over the pictorial space. Cadmium
orange or stripes brightened with white lift the
monochrome sky out of the background.

The painter-driver exploits his dual personality for
the benefit of the observer. In some instances the
view of the highway vanishing is isolated and boxed
in a single flat square of the picture plane. Geometry
is no longer the handmaiden of images; images are the
raiments of tectonics. Tuned to speed, geometry of
the barriers set crosswise over the view divides the
picture into "musical" sections. (This optical illusion
is actually due to the pull exerted by the vivid oblique
red stripes.) D'Arcangelo's shift of emphasis from distance to plane is an escape from the narrowing speed.
Relief from significant forms is in forms upset.

D'Arcangelo goes on to upset the order of images. In a recent painting, *Map*, which takes precedence, the image of the road or the map? The curve of the East Coast or the curve of the highway? The division of the painting into four equal squares or the content of the squares? In the beginning was the printed image. Then came the painting created in the image of its maker.

Another, more recent, series of highways are seen perpendicular. They confront the driver with his phobia: the road before him, climbing steeply over the next hill, suddenly rises and becomes a wall. Motion is paralyzed, feelings turn cold. What but anxiety can be expressed by the highway's white divide tapering toward the narrowest of skies in the bluest of nights? Barnett Newman was the first to have presented our world with a linear view of the ego. The exchange of ideas among artists is pursued in vivid dialogue that fearlessly transcends the great divide between the figurative and the abstract. What could be less nonabstract than the landscape of speed? Highways are not for pedestrians. Every mile of paved surface, with its lawn embankments, its framing trees, must be swiftly by-passed. Velocity subtracts. Painters reinterpret cutups into the new abstract-like compositions. The unreality of a glossy postcard's view is collaged to the schematic design of the highway; the green of the lawn is reappraised in terms of a vertical rectangle, the texture of grass is represented by a drawing on a ground rectangle; the sky, reduced to a tiny blue square substituting for the postcard's embellished view of dirt. The faint clouds of a heavenly summer day emerge from the Kodachrome blue of the card to roll in thick circles over parts of the unpainted canvas. In yet another work, the black surface of the highway is treated as a cutout and appears to be standing on its side when conjoined to the schematic drawing of an unfinished highway. In the dis-

Allan D'Arcangelo: *Proposition 30*, 1967. Acrylic on canvas. 9' x 9'. Photograph courtesy of Fischbach Gallery, New York.

tance the incomplete section of the road runs into a finished one, this time a ready-made ten-cent shiny reproduction of a curved road.

With the mechanization of the landscape the real and artificial blend and clash their respective colors, lights, and shapes. D'Arcangelo excels in the cross-fertilization of the abstract and the vernacular, the blueprint and the chromatic, the crowded postcard and the spacious canvas. The effects can be stunning.

In a recent series of "roads," D'Arcangelo increased the distance between reality and its abstract rendition by reducing the highway landscape to a broad central green band placed between two narrow bands, a blue one above and the other below forming a geometric black-and-white pattern. At times the sky itself forms a "road" dividing the green plane in two, at others a road sign set against the green makes the work appear particularly "abstract." These paintings are remarkably attractive; they fascinate the viewer much the way the road stretching before him fascinates the driver. It would seem relevant here to distinguish between "attractive abstraction" and "bland abstraction." With the former we are reminded of the Quattrocento true perspective which charms us with its compressed distance betwen foreground and background, of Chirico's false projects of cubes which heighten the illusion of mystery, of Mondrian's subtraction of the image from a divinely divided space. With D'Arcangelo, the narrow space encasing the driver has been banished from the roadway, the omission compensated by the vastness of green.

Some critics have denied that D'Arcangelo's highroads are genuine Pop Art because they are not two-dimensional. Confound the wise! How much longer are we to be told that more is less? Painting is more than the eye can see.

D'Arcangelo, in paintings of 1967, got off the highway by making a left turn. Yet he remains in the driver's seat: what he sees on his left differs from what lies on his right. What the viewer sees is an abstract painting supported by a highway vocabulary. In the oversize *Landscape*, 1967 (38 inches by 42 inches), and in the small *American Landscape* (9 inches by 19 inches), stripes have been lifted off the ground to rise and curve a path into the sky while a road sign stops a quatrefoil cloud. The landscape has been exploded, its parts swiftly reassembled; precarious compositions are firmly balanced by a vibrant curve, forcing the road's vanishing point to boomerang into a low summit. Arrows pointing skyward guide the driver in the direction of two-dimensionality.

With these paintings D'Arcangelo makes a most lively contribution to Expressionist geometry. This is a style, mannerist and centrifugal, that at present challenges systemic abstraction.

Allan D'Arcangelo: *Landscape*, 1967. Acrylic on canvas. 60" x 54". In the collection of Mr. and Mrs. Louis A. Lerner. Photograph courtesy of Fischbach Gallery, New York.

SUBJECT MATTER IN THE WORK OF
BARNETT NEWMAN*

Barnett Newman's series of monochrome fields divided
from top to bottom by a vertical line, when first shown
in 1950 (at the Betty Parsons Gallery), struck this
writer as a major artistic achievement. At last an artist
had come forth to state in an abstract style that the
Being is an "all in the now."

Statements do not have to be explained; they must
be understood. Gazing at a *kouros* we feel the impact
of Parmenides's dictum that man is an "all in the
now." The *kouros*, Hermes or Apollo, is the image of
idealized man. In our time the Being who sees himself
as an "all in the now" is agnostic, and views his solitude as inherent to the condition of man. Let us compare the advancing *kouros* to Giacometti's dissolving
figure to understand more fully the difference between
Parmenides and Kierkegaard. Both the ancient statue
and the modern one belong in a limited space. The
Apollo advances toward us from the depth of a cella
encased in a jewel-like temple. (To our mind's eye
even a ruined temple is a self-contained entity in
the now of sunrays.) The sense of remaining within
clearly defined grounds is epigrammatically expressed
in modern terms by Mondrian. How carefully he
located the position of a chosen one in a tiny rectangle of color!

In a series of paintings called *Onement*, Barnett

* Reprinted from *Arts Magazine*, November, 1967.

Newman separates the Now into left and right.[1] But who in the Now can assume the responsibility of dividing space into two separate parts, a left one and a right one? Only one who has doubted that the all is in the Here.

The sensation that the Now spreads beyond the finite is suggested in Sung paintings where the human figure is engulfed in an endless space, one which for the Taoist constitutes the absolute reality. Were Barnett Newman an orientalizing Westerner he would not have chosen the Fourteen Stations of the Cross as subject matter for his latest paintings, nor would he have written for their exhibition at the Guggenheim Museum his comments on the meaning of the last words of Jesus.

Perhaps Barnett Newman's poetic dissertation on the theme could be dismissed, since he freely acknowledges that the relation of his work to the Passion of the Cross occurred to him only after he had started painting the Fourth in this series.[2] This position would involve a refusal to view Picasso's *Guernica* in relation to the city's bombing on the grounds that the painting had been started before the disaster of Guernica. But the artist works by association, not chronologically.

To the fourteen paintings of the Passion of the Cross begun in 1958 and completed in 1966 we should add Newman's sculpture *Here II* of 1965. It consists of three thin metal verticals solidly implanted in individual trapezoid mounts on a common ground. They appear as acephalous crosses, since, no transversal

[1] In some works the pictorial plane is divided horizontally. These are less convincing, for they suggest landscapes rather than portraits, with the implication that the line dividing land and sky should be curved.

[2] This part of his statement, which appeared in *Art News*, May, 1966, was not included in the catalogue to his exhibition at the Guggenheim Museum.

Barnett Newman: *Here II*, 1965. Steel. In the collection
of Philip Johnson.

bars limit their upward thrust. It is as if Barnett Newman was saying that we are not "all in the now."

Most movingly King David conveys the idea that
man is not all in the now when he exclaims in Psalm
22: "My God, my God, why hast Thou forsaken me?
. . . I cry in the daytime, but Thou hearest not; and in
the night season, and am not silent." For the Psalmist,
man is not at all in the now because the now is part
of eternity. When the Crucified Jesus repeated, "My
God, why hast Thou forsaken me?" his followers interpreted these words as the outcry of a human being
who is simultaneously mortal and immortal, in the
Now and in Eternity and never all in the Here.

Newman's crosses have not been contained in the
Here by lines stretching out like arms across the
horizon. Newman's crosses are crossless, since the
cross, besides being the symbol of the crucified, is also
the emblem of a God. Barnett Newman identifies himself with the agony of a compassionate man who was
crucified, not with the transfiguration of a mortal
being. Acephalous crosses are for those who have been
cut off from the hope of immortality. In the Now,
man is alone. His cry for help cannot reach the Above,
for there is no above and no beyond. Man is alone in
the Now.

In his statement on the Stages of the Passion Barnett
Newman says: "*Lema Sabachthani*? Why did you
forsake me? Why forsake me? To what purpose? Why?
This is the Passion. This outcry of Jesus. Not the
terrible walk up the Via Dolorosa, but the question
has no answer." David spoke in anguish because he
was not hearing the voice of God: "My God . . . I cry
in the daytime, but Thou hearest not, and in the night
season, and am not silent." In the night the agony
grows worse, for we do not see. For the poet-painter,
convinced of his solitude, an agonizing situation is best
evoked through an awareness of the limitations of
sight: "I do not see because it is too dark to dis-

tinguish objects; I do not see because nothing is there. I do not see because all is black. I do not see because all is blank." Unable to see he feels out of place. Through the will to see what canot be seen he reaches a point where he finds himself in ecstasy—a word that means out of place.

In the hour of crisis no right place can be found; we waver, doubt, shift position from left to right and back again.

The engaged viewer watches for variations in the series of fourteen paintings: the expansion or contraction of the white/black areas, the increase or decrease of verticals, the reversal of the left to right movement. Jesus's Passion begins when he knows that he is condemned. The Fourteen Stages of his Passion could be represented by fourteen states of ecstasy. From the moment we know ourselves to be lost we are in ecstasy and out of place in the Here, albeit still in the Now.

Suspended between life and death is an experience that can be communicated to others in terms of an insoluble black and white contradiction. Ecstasy is a confrontation with reality: in ecstasy there is no room for illusion, everything has to be reduced to an immediacy felt in the tension between lines and planes, raw canvas and/or white and black surfaces, or twilight zones of gray.

Twelve out of fourteen of Newman's Stations are divided into four by vertical lines. Like Zurbarán with his twelve pictures of the Apostles, Newman is a master of serialization. We move back and forth from Station One to Station Fourteen, enriching our understanding of each painting through confrontation with the others. Sometimes the strongest side of the painting lies on the left, occupied by a vast area buttressed by a forceful margin, while a narrow median line divides vertically the plane into unequal sections. Sometimes the divided plane is more clearly

Barnett Newman: *Thirteenth Station*, 1966, of *The Stations of the Cross: Lema Sabachthani.* Acrylic polymer on canvas. 78″ x 60″. Photograph courtesy of The Solomon R. Guggenheim Museum, New York.

visualized as an uninterrupted ground upon which two verticals have been traced. The combination of two vertical lines and one plane evokes the Trinity, while the double set of two lines and two planes recalls the Pythagorean tetractys. The position of the signature varies: in some it is placed in the lower left corner, in others in the lower right, and in a few at some distance from the end. Some lines are blurred, others vertically subdivided. In Station Four, the black bleeds, falling on the immaculate plane in a shower. In Station Five, the black margin is torn by spreading Expressionist stains. In Station Twelve tears and trembling shake the right end with delicate convulsions. Man can rise above his destiny and face the impossible. Black is set against white, black and white confront us with the dullness of raw canvas. Black lifts the raw canvas to the purity of white.

What is the painter trying to see? What else but light? The poet knows that the word is light. So is vision. Speech created man different from other species. Created man formed himself in the image of his God. Out of images we cannot make flesh. Out of sound the musician cannot create solidity. Out of colors the artist cannot bring forth light. Barnett Newman added a fifteenth painting to the series. In it he contrasts the orange of dawn to the blackness of night by a thin margin on the left and a thin margin on the right.

The Impressionists were the first to isolate light, and the Abstract Expressionists the first to isolate existence. Pollock and de Kooning achieved their goal by reducing painting to a handwriting of gestures, and Barnett Newman by reducing the image to a divided monochrome field. To the Expressionist's calligraphy of gestures he opposes the typography of the vertical. Handwriting is personal, typography impersonal. Pleasure can be found both in deciphering the expression and in detecting variations in repetition. Through series of gestures the Existentialist expresses himself; through the repetition of stereotypes the Empiricist manifests himself.

After being viewed for so long as a pioneer of Expressionism, Barnett Newman emerges as a forerunner of systemic art.

Systemic painting substitutes redundancy for contradiction. In the Stages of the Cross, despite the repetition of the pattern fourteen times, the antithesis between white and black areas, narrow and broad fields, strong and weak lines, is never annihilated. Each painting is at a climax. An image of tension is lifted by the mind from the surface where lies that literal meaning scribes excel in describing. And what Jesus thought of scribes is well known.

ALEX KATZ: FACES AND FLOWERS *

Through the years Alex Katz's portraits have grown larger and larger. His most recent heads are about six to seven times the normal size. Does this make them less real than had they been merely double the size? What is more real, a portrait that is too large or too small? In his *Pensée sauvage* Lévi-Strauss explains how Clouet, searching to preserve the clarity of reality, in his small-scale portraits avoided reproducing all the details of a collar. The smaller-than-size portrait is easily dominated by the viewer and, if he is its owner, he can enjoy the feeling that it is absolutely his. Conversely, a Pantocrator's image spread over an entire dome crushes the worshippers by its vast presence. In their severity Katz's giant portraits tangentially evoke the austere Byzantine mosaics. The Christ in Majesty had his traits broadened and elongated in conformity with architectural considerations. Clouet's and Holbein's contracted portraits corresponded to the ever more intimate atmosphere of the private homes of humanists.

Viewed in relation to our modern living rooms, Katz's portraits are oversized. The living room serves as middle ground between the self and the world. Some years ago Katz painted a series of windows from within the room: those look abstract because he subtracted the middle ground. Our lasting impression is

* Reprinted from *Art International*, November, 1967.

of delightful colored patterns formed by light seen through the window.

It is not a coincidence that the modern oversize painting is traceable to Matisse's *Studios*. The studio is a workroom, and work is either secret or public, not private. The oversize painting is expansive rather than contracted, seductive rather than reflective, and opened to the world. The oversize picture is a slow exaggeration: it delays understanding. It takes scanning from all sides to uncover its significance.

Katz enriched the expansive style practiced by the younger artists of our day with portraits of faces and flowers taken from life and not from lively magazines and ads. This group of artists looks at nature and picture books fed by a memory packed with abstract patterns.

Unlike blown-up photographs, Katz's giant portraits are clear and precise, yet never harsh as are billboard faces. By a subtle interplay of halftones Katz endows his faces with a wealth of variations. He paints a large picture with all the care that must be put into a small one. He handles each area of color with the attention that an old master would give to jewels and brocades.

In his portrait of the poet Kenneth Koch, Katz has built up the resemblance out of irregular shapes designed by the interplay of light and dark tones of artificial pinks. He has subtracted all delineation from the face's middle ground. The contrast between nose and cheek, neck and jaw is produced by colors only, not by lines. Katz stresses geometric properties of features in post-Cubist and strictly coloristic terms. Abstract considerations determined the size of Koch's eyes. Each one is reduced to a set of three circles, iris, pupil, and spot of light, and enlarged then with glasses reinforced by eyebrows. This relatively heavy construction is supported by an ideal triangle that has the parted lips for basis and for apex the bridge of the glasses. An asymmetric contour adds character to the face. The painter brings light and transparency to the non-existent glass by depicting literally the reflection with whitish vertical lines set over the eyes. Were it not for these patterns of light in the eye and over the face, the portrait would not have been brought to life. Is it not by the absence of brightness that we recognize death at a glance?

Katz's portraits remain impenetrable. This painter shuns the intimate, and sacrifices expression to concentrate on presence which is impersonal and public. It is the oversize publicity portraits that become prototypes of personalization.

Some of Katz's most striking works are overlapping double portraits. Katz presumably resorts to this technique to dramatize differences in personality traits, not to suggest depth, as did the Egyptians. In *Ada and Vincent*, his wife and son, the artist focused his attention on the two pairs of eyes. These have the same peculiarities: the right eyelid of both mother and child forms an angle, while the left one is rounded. Both have dark eyes, but, unlike his mother who looks out of the picture with calm and self-confidence, the boy, with childish uncertainty, denoted by the slightly uncoordinated gaze, avoids the viewer. He seems content to be under the protection of his mother, to feel on his cheek the warmth of the hand resting on his shoulder and, probably too, the tenderness of a kiss. Both faces have been modulated by a tonal interplay, the mother's brightened and the child's caressed by shadows, for the light falls between the two, illuminating hers. It is the mother's hair that casts a shadow over part of her dress, deepening its red. We are charmed by such details and intrigued by the composition, by the two cropped ovals, one enfolding the other.

The double portrait of *Lara and Alain Jacquet* (the

Alex Katz: *Ada and Vincent,* 1966. Oil on canvas. 95″ x 72″. Photograph courtesy of Fischbach Gallery, New York.

painter) violates the rules formulated by Gestalt psychologists to distinguish a good overlapping from a bad one. Alain's profile covers such a small area of the girl's lovely face that it is impossible to visualize the two heads as forming a harmonious composite whole. Katz's purpose is to stress the shape and draw attention to the color of the girl's eyes, and to minimize the roundness of the face. By cutting into her eye, he has established a peculiar balance between the three eyes. The faces differing from each other in tonality only, and freed from outlines, our attention is drawn to the contrast between the physical closeness of the lovers and their personal isolation. This double portrait might be seen as the complementary opposite of Brancusi's *Kiss*.

Katz's faces are typical, his flowers botanical. He creates floral patterns that are to the abstract artist's geometry of colors what Gothic design is to the Greek. The more we look at Katz's lilies and daisies, the clearer we see an abstract pattern emerging from what at first seemed a plain floral composition. In *Violet Daisies #2* four flowers fill the picture, their petals and leaves playing with tones of violet and tones of green against a field of yellow in support of flower heads of a different yellow. Viewed in terms of composition, the picture is divided into two parts by an ideal oblique line—suggested by fingerlike leaves pointed downward, separating as it were the bottom flowers from those above. The tonal play together with the overlappings of petals and leaves scatter our attention. This is pleasantly disconcerting, distracting the eye from resting on any particular flower. The floral theme has been used to structure a surface that has to be visualized in terms of a single indeterminate pattern consisting of subtle variation of a floral phrase.

We have an indeterminate pattern again in *White Lilies* set against a dark field. The picture is divided

Alex Katz: *Violet Daisies* #1, 1966. Oil on canvas. 48″ x 32″. Photograph courtesy of Fischbach Gallery, New York.

in two by a diagonal half hidden by lilies shaping an empty space into a U, pictorially balanced by the leaves filling the empty space of the lower left corner.

Superb Lilies #2 is a spectacular study of abstract patterns formed by three tiger lilies, folding petals into crowns, stretching sheaves of pistils into curving rays. The variations on this theme are kept under control by an underlying geometric structure consisting of three triangles. Those on the right and left have an upper corner of the picture for apex, while the central triangle has the basis of the other two for its sides. This subdivision brings to the fore the rich variations of the floral pattern, predominantly of petals and leaves in the left triangle, of overlapping curved petals in the right one, of curved petals and elongated pistils in the central triangle.

Blue Flag, with its tonal variations of purple and green, transforms a single flower into floral-shaped areas of color that with the intervening green spaces create a vibrant pattern startling and original.

Katz lifted realism out of an old textbook and abstract art out of studios, creating with these irreconcilables a vision enchanting and bright. To endure, works of art have to be enjoyed for themselves again and again. Viewed in the perspective of modern art's endless renewals, Katz's work marks a moment that is absolutely new.

THE ORIGINALITY OF AL HELD*

Abstract Expressionism made us aware of the necessity to distinguish between scale and size. Pollock's paintings are never large in the sense a Tintoretto or a Rubens are large. A Pollock is large the way Joyce's *Ulysses* is long. There is a difference, however; while *Ulysses* may seem endless because the reading time is filled with long descriptions of minute incidents, Pollock's *#1* is large because we view the whole without being aware that it is filled with fascinating details. Variations within interrupted and hyphenated lines, whether straight or curved, between lines and dots, specks of red or yellow, fall into a whole that could be seen as a field or stars of the heavens or the blades of grass in a meadow. With field painting there occurs a radical shift of emphasis from incomprehensible graphic signs to typical signs. Monet and Seurat had already reduced cathedrals and promenaders, haystacks and acrobats to Impressionistic interpretations of retinal effects. Field painters today reduce the organization of circles, parallels, chevrons, and dots to Impressionist effects of forms.

For its best effects Impressionism relies on vagueness—between objects and atmosphere, shape and form, pattern and field. Contrarily Expressionism cultivates distortions and provokes interruptions. Preoccupation with pattern is a central one in abstract art. Field painting subordinates pattern to scale. The

* Reprinted from *Art International*, May, 1968.

Al Held: *The Big A*, 1962. Acrylic on canvas. 10' x 14'. Photograph courtesy of Andre Emmerich Gallery, New York.

large format of an "empty" painting compels the observer to view it as a whole, undivided.

One of Seurat's major achievements was to have adapted the human figure which the Egyptians had fitted into a hieroglyphic layout to a layout involving dots in a pointilliste landscape with figures. Seurat corrected Piero della Francesca, who, wishing to enhance the moral and social nobility of his personnages, presented them on a scale slightly oversized compared to their quarters. Francesca's sense of grandeur was in our time exploited by Léger to serve the ideology of industry and labor. With Léger, Grecian bodily proportions are reappraised and blended to harmonize with engines. A sense of grandeur was thereby created, ignored by field painting and reintroduced by Al Held.

Like Impressionism, field painting tends to reduce painting to retinal effects. If its genuine discoveries are not to be dismissed, it will have to be challenged on its own grounds. Al Held does so by readjusting the use of scale. The example of Fernand Léger might have encouraged an abstract artist to make of scale the content of his painting. But for form not to remain a shape among shapes, as it does in Expressionism, for form not to remain a copy of a circle or a square, it has to be visualized as a specific object, a concrete thing presented on a scale that clashes with the scale of the picture plane. Whenever successful the results could be compared to those of the great mannerists, and lead to the discovery of new ways of incorporating unresolved tensions in orderliness.

In *The Big A* Al Held has subtly distorted the letter so that it could be mistaken for an irregular black quadrangle, the complementary opposite of the quadrangular field of white. This last impression needs correction when we become aware that the A is a field of black which includes three geometric figures, two shaped by the empty figures within the A, the third by the upper right corner. From this new vantage point we might wonder whether the A is not actually a black building, with a window open to light the sky. Or might it be a billboard-size letter? Let us call it an idiosyncratic letter. Perhaps we may best describe it as the A with the blue window and the white door, the way we describe a Madonna by Parmigianino as "The Virgin with the Long Neck."

The Yellow X. Were it not for its title could we have guessed the field of lemon yellow bitten into on all four sides by corners is a letter of the alphabet? Once the identification is made, it clings. Let us now ponder over the field of yellow. The deep cut on the left, the folded triangle on top, the notches on the two other sides give the field a singular crosslike appearance; yellow stone ready to fall, prevented from falling by the X irrevocably fastening the field to the four corners of the canvas.

Of all Held's letters *The Big N* is the most extreme. The spaces comprised between the bars of the N have been reduced to two dark notches, and the bars eliminated. The function of these notches is to fasten the field of white to the corners, not just to pin the field down, but to prevent it from changing with the size of the environment. This painting is a concrete thing; it is not a scale of measure; it pulsates with scale.

The Upside Down Triangle is upside down because it points downward and looks upward and inward. We must therefore see its inner white triangle as a plane lying back of the picture plane. Where, then, does order start and disorder end? Follow the tension; do not surrender to either order and the ideal of formalism, or to disorder and the romanticism of Expressionism.

In *Circle and Square* these basic forms are joined like two consonants of an unknown alphabet. They are drawn toward each other by their contrasting qualities, the narrowness of the red circle's border and

Al Held: *The Big N*, 1965. Acrylic on canvas. 9′ x 9′. Photograph courtesy of Andre Emmerich Gallery, New York.

Al Held: *Circle and Triangle*, 1964. Acrylic on canvas. 12′ x 28′. Photograph courtesy of Andre Emmerich Gallery, New York.

the width of the white triangle's black border. It is the broadness of the left side's field of red and the right side's field of white that prevents these shapes from forming a pattern, geometric or lettristic.

Ivan the Terrible is a T and an X, a dramatic close-up evoking Eisenstein's famous movie. More than any other art the cinema has conditioned us to accept the change of scale as natural. We have now to learn to take scale in our stride, in a Cubist stride, as did Eisenstein, as does Al Held.

The Red Seagull must have received its name after the work was completed. By identifying a triangle of red, topping a field of blue with a flying gull, Held shows that to reinforce a form he will not hesitate to bind its shape to an image. Form gives life to shapes and images. This the formalists will never understand, for they hate life.

Mao is one of Al Held's most impressive works. This picture is a thing, not an impression of things, of circles within circles whirling, of advancing or receding planes. By squaring his circle with four notches, Held has created the double portrait of the square and the circle. The notches point to the four corners of the picture, for they lie on its diagonals, stabilizing the relation between the two circles and the squares, compelling us to view the latter in terms of the picture plane rather than of superimposed planes. The narrow margins set above and below the field of blue tend to compensate for the relative narrowness of the upper and lower side of the circle which otherwise would appear oblong. By calling the picture *Mao*, Al Held stresses the concreteness or individuality of a picture whose face is no more a perfect circle than is Mao's face. Al Held makes objects; he does not elaborate optics. He prefers to enrich our mind with images than dazzle us with illusionistic tricks.

Greek Garden is like a gigantic frieze, its center occupied by a white square surrounded on three sides

Al Held: *Mao*, 1967. Acrylic on canvas. 9½′ x 9½′. Photograph courtesy of Andre Emmerich Gallery, New York.

by an enormous frame of black. On the left there is an irregular red circle framed in red, sinking like a sun; on the right there is a yellow triangle set in a huge truncated triangle. This frieze of forms and signs reads like an ambitious project, worthy of our great metropolis, its energy and its plans, often so cruelly mutilated. Projects and images are what we most need. Impressions and expressions are not enough. Feelings alone are too little and will alone too much.

Contradictions in scale present the artist with a new set of themes. Let it be recalled that the Greeks of the classical age transformed their friezes into epic songs through the cadence of bodily movements of men and gods keyed to the scale of human proportions. Despite their efforts, the Egyptians, the Assyrians failed to express convincingly the difference between human scale and the supernatural one of gods and deified men. Scale cannot reflect the supernatural. If the difference of scale is to be successfully applied, the nature of the support must replace nature, and the struggle between man and the superhuman machine must be signified by tensions and distortions.

VIII.
BETWEEN
SILENCE

* Poetry should be seen and not heard; music should be as hard as bones; painting should think.
* What art deforms art history reforms.
* If artists could only imitate their mistakes!
* The critic's barriers are the poet's bridges.
* The painter devoted to painting, the poet devoted to poetry are but craftsmen.
* Faith is worse than bad faith.
* To appreciate the art of lying, learn to listen.
* Inspiration: putting two and 2 together.
* The artist can create only one thing: his parents.
* The critic's role is to protect the artist from the public.
* Wanted: Fewer critics and more snake charmers.
* Wanted: Less clarity and more intensity.
* Plagiarism avoids imitating failure.
* Where there are no secrets there is no poetry.
* More alcohol and less prosody!
* Poetry is to painting what socialism is to labor.
* The poet's role is to pour images into prose; the artist's role is to pour poetry into art; the critic's role is to pour acid into prose.
* Proletarian goals, bohemian tastes, and mannerist manners.
* Museums in every block and curators in every drugstore!
* Supermen are for supermarkets and heroes are for sandwiches.

* St. Sebastian: the patron saint of the Hippies.
* Cholesterol is to butter what sonnets are to urns.
* Sea horses are the poodles of the sea waiting to see Venus eat noodles.
* If Christ is the Word He is the cross-word.
* Cortisone, the worst side effect since Eve.
* The hamburger: better red than dead.
* What if a hippodermic needle falls into the circus?
* Who can tell if William Tell ate or not the apple of his eye?
* Now that all the cats are square, only the fish say miaou.
* My steak is my dog's mistake.
* Parallels meet in the corner of anxiety, the corner-stone without the I.
* Christopher Columbus, great for having betrayed India.
* Democracy and quality should not be confused. Change the rule of the game: art courts chance. Let critics bow to Fortuna and cast the die. It fell on 3. He who got three votes is the winner. Choice is a matter of injustice, and conditioned by love or chance.
* If Adam had cut down the cherry tree and Washington had eaten the forbidden fruit, would Lenin have ever reached the Finland Station?
* Art must be explosive! Proof: the Parthenon.
* Let us oppose the schools of the Sepik River to the tribes of the Renaissance.
* The novel is the word made flesh.
* The More kinetic the sculpture, the more static the dance.
* After kinetic sculpture what?—Paralytic sculpture.
* The billboard is to Pop Art what the ceiling was to the Baroque.
* Marie Antoinette lost her scull because she was not pop.
* Reduce the gap between vanilla ice cream and

mayonnaise to a difference in temperature, and the art of cooking will have reached the drugstore.

* Marcel Duchamp: Picasso's guilty conscience.
* Mondrian: Veronica without the veil.
* Matisse curved color into odalisques.
* Martha Graham curved the backs of dancers à la Matisse.
* Mona Lisa's moustache is what Dali and Leonardo have in common.
* With Chirico the Gare Montparnasse becomes the point of departure back to Palladio.
* Dali is the authentic false Vermeer.
* Giacometti marks the exit of the kouros.
* With Kandinsky the rainbow becomes Faustian.
* With van Gogh's plow de Kooning unearthed Rubens.
* Henry Moore may think he made mountain-size statues when he produced only women-size mountains.
* Hopper: the bathetic fallacy.
* Hans Hoffman: his pupils' best pupil.
* Motherwell: big not Kline.
* Ad Reinhardt: Their darkest our.
* Jasper Johns hit the target; Noland circled it.
* Stuart Davis made Cubism jazzy; Lichtenstein makes it groovy.
* With Larry Poons the eye touches music.
* Matisse painted Magritte: Frank Stella illustrates Rose.
* Toni Smith: minus the pyramid plus minimal.
* Robert Morris: minisurreal and maximinimal.
* Olitski: Odilon Redon without the dream and Monet without the eye.
* Trova's charioteers of the highroad minus the ode.
* Noland: Linear C.
* Morris Louis: the tape recorder of mysticism.
* Morris Louis veiled the crucifix with smog colors.

* Tinguely: more kinetic than frenetic.
* Takis makes compasses to Nowhere.
* Pol Brui: kinetics of the low metabolism.
* Only Chryssa caught the firebird.
* Robert Whitman is the only true minimalist: he reduced line and color to a ray.
* Ray Johnson is the only tempting minimalist: he reduced line and color to a serpent.
* Moore is less. —And Marianne Moore?
* Clement Greenberg: the worst influence on art since Savonarola.
* A rose is a rose is a rose is not by Barbara Rose.
* Barbara: how does the minimal become maximal sub rose?
* Super Critics: Anal Isis and Miss Sticks.
* What is the role of the asymptote in symptomatic art?
* Nicolas Calas is in and out of art; Hilton Kramer is insight out.
* W. H. Auden began as the Byron of the proletariat and became the Pope of the Alexandrians.
* Wallace Stevens: the Faust of the BMT.
* Samuel Beckett: Am I lame in the left leg or in the right one?
* Lolita: a lepidopterist's view of Madame Butterfly.
* McLuhan mistook the transistor for the stone of philosophy.
* With Ivy Compton-Burnett logical positivism comes in a family-size package.
* Charles Olson: the bad breath of poetry.
* John Cage uncaged the sound of ages.
* I do not write to be read but to be reread.